White Elephants

a memoir

by Chynna T. Laird

Eagle Wings Press
Imprint of Silver Boomer Books
Abilene, Texas
www.EagleWingsPress.com

Published by Eagle Wings Press,
    imprint of Silver Boomer Books,
3301 S 14th Suite 16 - PMB 134, Abilene Texas 79605

ISBN: 978-0-9826243-2-6

Printed in the United States of America

Table of Contents

White Elephants

An Introduction

While the White Elephant is an esteemed possession in India, valued as an asset, the costs of upkeep greatly exceed its usefulness and ownership ultimately becomes a liability.

I always knew there was something different about my mother, Janet. But I never saw her behavior as "wrong." I grew up in the '70s, after all, and during that time almost everyone acted just like my mom, right? Impulsive, "hippie-like," and ready to party. It wasn't until I hung out at my friends' houses and saw how those families functioned and interacted with one another that I realized life in my house may not have been quite as normal as normal should have been.

Perhaps people felt there was nothing more they could do, you know? After all, how can someone be helped who doesn't see the need? A Christian counselor I saw for a while described such situations as, "a White Elephant everyone can see but no one wants to deal with; everyone hopes the problem will just go away on its own."

Just like with my mom.

Back then it seemed women were almost expected to go a little loopy sometimes. After all we're the ones with raging hormones that get out of whack – by our periods, PMS or pregnancy and childbirth – and cause craziness and bizarre behavior. And because of those uncontrollable hormones, women are also more emotional and predisposed to depression. These are things my mom was actually told by her parents, her family, her husbands and friends...even her doctor. Eventually, she made herself believe that her erratic behavior stemmed from PMS, not mania or alcohol.

Another factor of my mother's situation was that she was adopted shortly after birth. Adoptions were closed back in the 1950s. That meant you pretty much got what you got "as is." No access was allowed to family health history, so adoptive parents could not be warned of susceptibility to mental illness.

If anyone had been curious enough to investigate these facts in my mom's situation, they may have found that her mother was bipolar and alcoholic, too. Hmmm...so, why didn't anyone try to find out these things about my mom or help her? I guess no one wanted to take on the responsibility.

If my own mental state had deteriorated to the point where I'd hurt myself or those around me, I would have wanted the assurance that someone would have been brave enough to have forced me into treatment. And it angered me as a woman, a mother, a sister, a friend, a lover, and a daughter, that people didn't do more to help my mother – that I didn't do more.

I wished those around Mom knew how to help her; or were willing to help her, or even to help her help herself. Nobody was brave enough to take that first step. Doing so would have meant taking on total responsibility – for my brother and me and my mom's situation. Well, nobody wanted that. Not even me.

There's a psychological term for that. Deindividuation. You know, where everyone thinks someone else will do something but no one does a thing? Never mind. It doesn't matter now. What matters now, at least to me, is that no matter what my mom did or didn't do, no one was brave enough to grab her hand. But I'm taking it now and raising it up.

Janet Batty was a person with mental illness. It doesn't excuse the things she did or erase the damage done as a result of some of her bad choices. But her story can help others. It might give strength to those who see a mother, sister, daughter, lover, wife, best friend, teacher or acquaintance in need.

PART I:

TALES FROM
YOUNG EYES

Chapter One

Little Girl Lost

Lukewarm acceptance is more
bewildering than outright rejection.
~ Martin Luther King, Jr. (1929-1968)

My younger brother Cam and I spent a lot of
time with our grandparents when we were
children. By a lot of time I mean there were
stretches – sometimes days, sometimes weeks –
when our grandparents cared for us. Grandma
Batty called such visits "Mom's vacations."

I used to think, *Wow, being a piano and
singing teacher must be an awesome job if she
can go on vacation so much!* Then I decided my
mother couldn't have been going on very fun
vacations since no one ever talked about them.
There were never any pictures or souvenirs from
those vacations, like when Grandma went to
Hawaii. Whenever Cam or I asked questions or
tried talking about the vacations, we were told,

"Your Mom is just going through a rough time. She'll be okay in a few days." I was never satisfied with that answer.

At five years old, I was way too curious for my own good, at least that's what I was told. I was one of those kids who just needed to know things and wasn't afraid to ask the questions that made all the adults in the room shut up: "What's a 'rough time?'" "How long will she be okay before she needs to go away again?" "Why can't we go with her?" "Why do you put those bottles away when Mom is here?"

Questions like those made my grandmother's lips purse, her face turn red. Then she'd say something like, "You know, you're far too curious. It comes from your strawberry blonde hair and your Scottish background. You let us worry and ask the questions, thank you very much."

I'm not sure what my hair color had to do with my "feistiness" (another Grandma-ism). I think not knowing or understanding things drove me nuts, so if people weren't going to tell me what I needed to know, I took the initiative to figure things out on my own – even if it meant listening in, spying, or taking things apart.

At five, I also realized things were more serious than my grandparents let on. I had a feeling that I was being left out of the big secret everyone else around me knew.

I stomped my foot and shouted at Grandma one evening before bedtime. "Why won't you just tell me what's going on?" It was the second week of the latest "vacation" and I wanted to know where Mom was. Or if she was even coming back.

Grandma never even looked up from her knitting. "Curiosity killed the cat, Tami. And don't stomp your foot at me again or you'll get a spanking."

I crossed my arms and glared. "You can't spank me. You're not allowed."

Grandma's knitting needles stopped mid-stitch. Her hazel eyes peered at me over her reading glasses. "Young lady," she said slowly, "I may not be your mother, but you are staying in this house, and you will follow our rules. I won't allow you to speak to me in that tone, do you understand me? I know you don't get the discipline you need at home but, by cracky, you'll get it here. Now go get ready for bed and I'll come tuck you in."

I considered stomping all the way to my bedroom but decided it wasn't a good plan. I did get an idea while I got ready for bed. I'd just have to make sure I listened in when Mom called my grandparents. Curiosity wasn't going to kill any cats at my grandparents' house, anyway. They had dogs.

Later that evening, I stirred awake at the sound of Grandma's voice. I snuck out of bed, tiptoed to the railing at the top of the staircase and heard my grandmother's loud whisper. It was the voice she used when talking about something interesting that the grandkids weren't supposed to hear. I just knew I had to listen in.

I slid the bedroom door closed so Cam wouldn't wake up and crept across the hall to the upstairs den, remembering to avoid the creaky boards right in front of the staircase, or the jig was up. I made it to the den door, then carefully dodged the small parcels of poop Grandma's dogs left. Clearing the booby-traps, I picked up the telephone extension, covered the receiver, and listened.

Grandma hissed, "Just when do you plan to come and get these kids, Janet? They're starting to ask where you are."

Mom's speech was slurred. "They don't care about me. You do a stupendous job at being their mom."

"Are you drinking?" Grandma asked.

"No," Mom said. "I already drank."

"You're supposed to be getting help. You come back here tomorrow and get these kids. You take some responsibility. Dad and I aren't going to be parents to your children."

For a good five seconds all I heard was the sound of the old pipes in the house creaking and clanking. I stared at the receiver with a furrowed brow. Then I heard crying.

"Don't start," Grandma said. I heard her slap the phone table. "Just get back here and be a mother to your children. They need you. Why can't you understand that? If you can't pull yourself up by the bootstraps for you, can't you do it for them?"

Mom sobbed. "I don't want them. Why don't you keep them? Please. Take them. I can't take care of them. Besides, they're better off without me."

Grandma's voice deepened. "I won't listen to any more of this. I'm telling these kids that their mother will be here tomorrow to get them. And you'd better be here or we'll just bring them to you."

A loud whisper from behind startled me, "What are you doing?"

It was Cam.

"Shhh..." I said, waving frantically at him. "Be quiet. If Grandma hears us..."

My eyes widened as I realized the receiver wasn't covered. Just before I slammed the phone on the cradle, I heard Grandma ask, "What was that?"

I grabbed Cam's hand, scanned the floor for the clearest path out and ran back to our room. As we sped past the staircase I heard Grandma say, "Wilf, go up and check on the kids. I think they heard us."

"Get back into bed and pretend you're asleep, Cam," I said, jumping into my own bed.

"What for?" Cam asked.

I rolled my eyes and gritted my teeth, "Just do it!"

We pretended to sleep as Grandpa thundered up the stairs and pushed our door open. A few seconds later I heard the bedroom door slide shut. The room was silent except for the occasional car whizzing down the main street behind my grandparents' house and Cam's rhythmic breathing.

I rolled over onto my stomach and smushed my face into my pillow, gripping it with both hands. As I cried, I wanted to believe it was the alcohol that induced Mom's words. I had to believe it was the alcohol.

I don't want them.
The words rang in my ears.
That's the night my heart first broke.

Breakfast was pretty quiet the next morning. Grandpa didn't make eye contact with us. As Cam and I ate our toast, grapefruit, and cereal with honey drizzled in the shape of the first letters of our names, Grandpa whistled away like nothing was wrong.

Between bites of toast I wanted to ask what was going on with my mom, but I couldn't. I frowned up at Grandpa. He looked back down at me with a little smile. He had such a kind face: deep blue eyes, chiseled cheekbones and strong jawline with a glimmer of the dimples we got to see when we'd make him laugh. I eased when he gripped my shoulder. I guessed that answered my unasked question. His gesture said, *"We know, Tam. This is the way it has to be. But we're here when things get too bad. And we love you."*

Despite what I'd heard and what I saw, I loved my mother. And I knew somewhere inside her bruised and tortured heart, our mom loved us, too. But my trust for her weakened with each vacation, after each telephone conversation and with every unanswered question.

I just wished I understood where her pain came from, and why she'd be okay one day, then take off the next. From that vacation on, I became determined to figure out what was going on, no matter what it cost or how much it hurt. Even if it made my grandparents angry with me; even if they cut off all my hair so the color of it would stop making me so curious; even if I got spankings or was grounded; or even if Mom didn't like me anymore...we deserved to know what was going on.

To me, it hurt a lot more not knowing, not understanding.

I held to that theory until she came to get us.

That next day was Sunday. We went to church every Sunday: Grandma's orders. Mom was even in the church choir! I'm not clear whether it was because they were devoted Christians or that our family simply needed to maintain a certain social appearance. But everyone had to be in church on Sunday mornings – no matter what went on the night before, at least when Mom wasn't on her vacations. When she was on her vacation, Cam and I still had to go. Nobody ever asked where Mom was, though.

Most of the people who went to church seemed to be the same age as Grandma and Grandpa. Everyone was dressed in Sunday best – gentlemen in suits, ladies in dresses and big flowery hats – and on their most polite behavior.

"How do you do, Mrs. So-and-So?"

"Oh, just fine, Mrs. So-and-So."

Cam and I endured lots of pinched cheeks, pats on the heads and hugs from the huggers who knew we were Lillian and Wilf Batty's grandchildren. It seemed to me people were much more interested in the social aspect of church than what the minister said.

We always sat in the middle pews. Cam and I were quickly divided because, for some reason, we always caught the giggles during the sermon. One Sunday, after a few unforgivable giggle-fests, I was wedged between Grandma and Grandpa with Cam stuck on the other side of Grandma. As the minister droned on with his sermon, I snuggled up to Grandpa's chest and lifted my eyes up, high above the choir loft to the stained glass window of Christ and His disciples.

I never knew why, but whenever I locked eyes with Christ, I felt a warm tide build in the pit of my stomach then spread out to my extremities. It was...calming. He sat on a stool, surrounded by His Disciples. The artist magically captured some of the Disciples' personalities in their expressions: Thomas' face was filled with doubt – his eyebrows raised in question; ever-devoted John rested his head in Christ's lap; and Judas faced away from Christ, guilt etched into his brow.

The scene was familiar for some reason, but it would be years before I truly understood its significance. I simply enjoyed the fullness in my heart when I looked into His sparkling aqua-marine eyes before dozing off.

In my lowest moments, there were three things I credited for keeping me and my hopes alive: Grandma and Grandpa's love; the undying devotion of Uncle Craig, Mom's younger brother; and that stained glass window.

I saw each of their faces – those from the stained glass window and my family – many times in my life. Each of them saved me in a profound way and reminded me that no matter what happened to my body, my soul would remain intact.

It had to.

Chapter Two

Loss of Innocence

Of all earthly music that which
reaches farthest into heaven is the
beating of a truly loving heart.
~ Henry Ward Beecher (1813-1887)

Well, Mom finally showed up to collect us, as
ordered, the day after the phone call with
Grandma. I never knew whether my mom was
scared of Grandma or just respected her so
much she wanted to work hard to please her, but
when Mom screwed up, and Grandma called her
on it, Mom jumped to fix things...eventually.

Mom walked into my grandparents' kitchen
just after noon that day, while Grandpa, Cam
and I ate roast beef sandwiches and tomato
soup. Grandma stood at the counter making
Grandpa another sandwich. She kept her back
to Mom for the first few minutes.

"Hey, everyone," Mom said in a squeaky, Minnie Mouse pitch. She wore oversized, dark brown sunglasses, jeans and a white t-shirt. Her hair was pulled back into a ponytail. I still wasn't sure where she'd gone on vacation, but I noted that she didn't even have a tan. *Strange,* I thought, *for a woman who got color in her skin standing out in the sun for only half an hour.*

"Just in time for lunch," my grandmother said, still facing the counter. "Sandwich?"

Mom shoved her sunglasses up on top of her head. "No, thanks. Not hungry. Just came to get the kids."

Grandma cleared her throat, then handed grandfather his sandwich. I shivered. Mom flopped herself on the chair beside me, threw her arms around my shoulders and pulled me into her. "I really missed you guys," she said, kissing my temple.

"Then why didn't you come sooner?" asked Cam. "We've been here forever."

I kept eating. So did my grandfather.

Mom pulled her arms away then leaned back into her chair. "Well, I was busy."

Cam frowned. "Busy? I thought you were on vacation? Aren't you supposed to have fun?"

Mom rubbed her palms on her thighs. That question made my grandmother turn around. Mom leaned forward, laughing, and mussed Cam's hair. "You ask the weirdest questions. Yeah, I had fun. But I was doing a few important things and have some great news for you two."

The good news was that Mom had found a new home for us: a three-bedroom townhouse in a rent-controlled community in Winnipeg. That meant the utilities were paid for, and the rent wouldn't go up much, if at all. The tenants consisted mostly of the working poor and military families; the Army base was within walking distance.

So, after lunch we grabbed our bags and Mom took us to tour our new home. It wasn't bad. The community was jam-packed with kids, there was a park nearby, and we could walk to our grandparents' house. Mom seemed much happier with her own space there. She even took on a few piano students. But not too long after we'd settled in, she was having trouble paying the bills and was forced to face a part of her past: our father.

It was the first time since their divorce they had met face to face. Apparently, Dad had written us letters from his military post in India. He had taken a lot of out-of-country postings to cope with losing us. I didn't remember reading or receiving any letters but remembered beautiful gifts Mom had received. One particularly memorable gift was a statue of a gorgeous Indian woman with long, dark hair. The doll was dressed in a striking blue and silver traditional Indian outfit, authentic right down to the jewel between her eyes and the diamond in her nose. She even balanced a water jug on her head. The details were stunning – the little jug was real clay. The most ironic thing was that the Indian woman looked so much like my mom.

At barely over five feet tall, my mother wasn't exactly a runway model. On top of being very short, she had what she called "football shoulders" and a stocky torso. Let's just say she didn't wear strapless dresses or tops very often. She used to joke that she was a great person to have on a football team because she could run fast and tackle hard...for a girl. So it wasn't really her body that boys were attracted to, but she had an exotic beauty and magnetic personality that captured attention.

Mom had a perfect oval-shaped face. Her hair was black and waist-length and always so shiny. It reminded me of Grandma's black lacquered baby grand piano. Her eyes were a deep emerald with flecks of gold and her black eyebrows perfectly shaped around them. She had a small nose and tiny lips, but boy, did she have the biggest, whitest teeth you've ever seen! When she smiled, people always said something like, "Oh my God, Janet. It's a wonder that you aren't an Osmond sibling!" Her olive skin made it look like she had a permanent tan, even in the winter. And the one thing that always sticks out in my mind when I think of her is that she liked going barefoot – even in the coldest weather. She loved flipflops, sandals and open-toed shoes. It's funny what you remember...

So, the visit with Dad didn't go very well. Because we hadn't seen him in over three years, and Mom never talked about him, we had no idea who he was.

The scene played out like this: "Okay, let's get you guys cleaned up," Mom said, after we'd finished a snack of peanut butter and strawberry jam sandwiches. She was chain smoking and twirling her hair. "Your dad is coming to see you."

I reached down and grabbed Cam's hand. "I don't want to wash up again. We look fine to me." Cam had jam squished around his mouth and on the front of his shirt.

Mom shoved us toward the bathroom while she spoke, a cigarette dangling from the side of her lips. "Don't be silly, Tam. I want him to see how good everything is. C'mon. Go wash up. And get that stuff off Cam's face and shirt."

She was all dressed up and smelled like perfume, so I knew it was serious. The doorbell rang. After a few minutes, she squealed something, then called us down. "Tam. Cam. Come here. You guys have a visitor."

Cam didn't want to go downstairs – he was terrified. So, Mom told Dad to "...go on up. They'll be so excited."

The visitor we had just learned was "Dad" came to Cam's room, where we sat on the bed with our arms around one another. He seemed to know us. "Well, hi there, you guys," he said. "Can I come in?"

He wore a blue uniform with wings on the sleeves and a matching beret. He stood in the doorway with an armful of presents and a big goofy grin – just like Cam's. I frowned at him as he handed me a plain wrapped gift. "Here ya go, Sweetie. God, you look just like your mother." His eyes brimmed with tears.

He scared me. I don't know whether it was his uniform that bothered me or that I just didn't know who he was, but my body started shaking. I yelled, "No, I don't! I don't know you. And I don't want your presents."

Cam cried and buried his face in my side. Dad chewed on the inside of his lower lip. "That's fine. I'll just leave these here and you can open them later, okay?"

He backed out of the room with his palms raised like he was under arrest or something. I pulled Cam closer to me while Dad lowered his hands, then he stood in the hallway, staring at us. I frowned at Dad again. He waved at me then wiped his eyes as he disappeared down the stairs.

"They don't even know who I am," he yelled at Mom. I covered my ears, knowing I'd pay for our reaction to him.

"What do you expect when you take off for almost three years without even making contact with them?" Mom asked.

Dad's voice got louder. "I did contact them. Didn't you read them my letters? Don't you even talk about me?"

Mom sputtered at him. Her shaky voice said, "Yeah. You're the Santa who sends them gifts for their birthdays and Christmas but nothing else."

"You sound just like your mother," he said. "You only asked me over here to squeeze money out of me. You won't even let me spend time with them. If you want more money, take me to court."

He called her some unrepeatable swear word I knew Grandma would have covered my ears from hearing. Mom swore back at him. The front door slammed. He was gone. After his tires squealed out of the driveway, I counted to 200 before going downstairs.

My mom was in the middle of the couch, leaning over with her head resting on her knees. Her long, black hair fell around her like a poncho. "Mom? Are you okay?" I finally asked.

She slowly sat up, strands of her hair sticking to her lips as she spoke. "Never mind. Just never mind. If he won't give us money, you're never going to see him again, you hear me? Not ever. We don't need him anyway. Forget him."

I didn't understand why Dad needed to pay her to see us. It sounded like an admission fee to the fair or the movie theater. It didn't sound right, but there was no way I was going to ask her about it.

"Strength" isn't a word I'd associate with my mom because she crumbled so easily under stress. "Determined," however, is a good description. Grandpa often called it "blind determinism" because Mom tried reaching a goal the fastest way possible without looking out for what land mines might be in her path. Maybe she managed to step over a few, but ultimately, fireworks exploded everywhere.

Whatever happened that day my dad stormed out on her sparked some of that determination in Mom. For a while after each crisis she forged ahead, perhaps trying to prove to everyone that she was fine and could take care of us, all by herself. She took on even more piano students while she practiced for her teacher's degree in music. She realized with a degree she could ask for more money from her students. And she was so good at piano, singing...and most other creative things.

No matter what else was happening, or how crappy the world was around her, Mom always had her music. Because I saw how much she loved music, I expressed an interest in it, and when we played together or when she gave me lessons, I got her full, adoring attention.

I played little songs, my feet dangling, seated next to my mother. I figured out how to read the little black dots with tails, as I called the notes, by watching her and listening to what she said to her students, "These are quarter notes: ta-ta-ta-ta; these are eighth notes: tee-tee-tee-tee."

I mustn't have been too bad for a five-year-old because I skipped all the irritating "Twinkle, Twinkle Little Star" baby stuff Mom usually made her students start with. I loved learning the more difficult pieces that needed both hands.

Though learning music from her was the best way to reach my mother, it became less and less fun as time went on – especially after she'd been drinking.

Music became what I turned to for comfort – I played piano to work through my emotions, or put on my headphones with Beatles blaring to tune things out for a while. Music was therapeutic for me.

Just as it had been for her.

Things became even more confusing for Cam and me. Much of the reason we weren't able to identify what was wrong was that there was no consistency or pattern in her drinking or her mania. Mom loved to party, but there would be long periods of time in between bouts of partying. Alcoholics Anonymous had a few commercials out at that time. They showed people called alcoholics drinking at work or hiding booze around their houses and drinking all day long every day, which wasn't my mother (at least not when we were young). She didn't fit neatly in that "alcoholic" category and, at the time, we didn't know anything about mental illness or bipolar disorder.

Then there was the fact that stuff happened all the time...oftentimes, really bad stuff – like when Mom would take off and leave us alone or hit us or get so sad that she'd tell us she wanted to die...but it was never talked about. We knew it happened. We saw it happen. We remembered everything, but somehow she either forgot what she did or just got used to the fact that nobody else seemed to remember what happened the night before.

A few months after the incident with Dad, Mom started dating a guy named Lyle. He wasn't a bad guy, but he sure loved his beer. He reminded me of Robert Redford in *Butch Cassidy and the Sundance Kid* with his yellowish-blond hair and matching bushy moustache. But Lyle's hair was wavy and shoulder-length, and he rarely had his shirt buttoned up past his pecs. He was a truck driver and, to put it bluntly, we seemed to be a pit stop for him. He came around for a month or so every few months, then he was gone again, but Mom seemed to really like him.

In the warmer months our neighbors had 'hood parties – what we called it when people hung out on their front stoops drinking. I think it was Lyle who started the custom. Our mother's participation at those parties seemed to become an annoyance to everyone. I think it was because she didn't seem to know when the party was over, especially when Lyle wasn't around. The neighborhood wives didn't like Mom throwing her perky young body in the faces of their forty-something husbands.

I rarely slept on 'hood party nights because the action happened on the neighbors' steps just to the right of my bedroom window. One party was the last straw for several stoopers. I knew Mom would find trouble that night, because she wore her cut-off shorts and a tube top. Lyle had been away longer than usual, and she'd been restless and nervous for almost a week. She bit her nails right down, smoked more than usual, wasn't able to sit still, and needed to be doing three things at the same time.

As the beer flowed, voices got louder, the tongues got looser, and laughter echoed longer. I didn't realize before these parties that curse words could be used not only in every possible tense but also as verbs, nouns, adjectives, pre-fixes...Geez, a curse word could even be some-one's name. (I hoped the guy named "Shithead," who was in charge of getting everyone's refill, would change his name later in life.)

I jolted awake to a scream so piercing I heard it even with my fingers in my ears and my pillow over my head. I tumbled out of bed and clambered onto the chair I had pushed earlier in the night to see out of my window. I figured it was late – the summer light had finally dimmed. But the street lamps gave enough light to see.

As I looked down, I saw the top of Mom's head disappearing into the front door below me, followed closely by the head of Muriel, one of the neighborhood wives.

I guessed Mom tried to slam the door, but Muriel managed to get in anyway.

"Get the hell out of my house!" Mom screamed.

There was a lot of stomping, a few more screams, then a dull thud. My heart pounded in my ears. I deduced Mom wasn't dead, because I still heard two voices.

Cam!

I tiptoed out of my room and peeked in his bedroom door. He was still asleep. I slid his window shut, closed his door, then went to the stairs to see what happened. I peeked over the wall of the staircase. Mom lay on the floor with each of her arms pinned under one of Muriel's chubby knees.

Muriel's face was two inches from Mom's, their noses almost touching. "Well, it's time for the neighborhood slut to reap what she sows," Muriel said. "You're gonna finally pay for what you stir up."

My mom had a terrible habit of hitting on her friends' husbands or boyfriends when she drank – something she never did when she was sober. It was a behavior that got her into a lot of trouble and ended many friendships.

"What are you talking about?" Mom asked, laughing. "I didn't do anything, I swear."

"Bull!" Muriel yelled, spitting all over Mom's face. "You flashed my husband and tried to get him to feel you up. I was standing right there. Do you think I'm stupid? You've been trying for weeks to start something with him. This ain't the Sixties anymore, Sweetheart."

My mother laughed again. "Your husband is the one who pulled down my top. Maybe you should yell at him. I have no control over your husband. Obviously you don't, either."

Whack! Muriel's meaty fist hit Mom's cheek. It sounded like someone slapping ground beef to make hamburger patties. I covered my eyes and cowered down behind the wall.

That smack seemed to shock some sense into Mom. "Oh my God, Muriel," she said, crying. "I swear, it was your husband's fault. I didn't do anything. Please stop. What about my kids?"

Muriel scoffed. "Oh. You remember your kids, then – those little darlings. I should call Social Services on you. Or better still, I should tell your mama what goes on around here. And I should tell that young boyfriend of yours what goes on when he's not around. You don't deserve to be a mom. You disgust everyone around here. You're nothing but white trash."

I peeked over the wall one last time to see if it was over. Muriel pushed herself up. "You stay away from my husband, you hear?" she said between gritted teeth. "You do anything like that to anyone else, and I'll come after you again. You hear me?"

As a final insult Muriel spat on Mom's chest, then she stormed out. Mom cried for several minutes. I waited until her cries softened to short hiccup-like breaths. Then I went to her and touched her arm. "Mom?" I whispered.

She rolled over. Her makeup ran down her cheeks making her look like a raccoon. She was covered in bruises, and the spit Muriel left behind ran down her side. She was pathetic. I knew it was her fault. I knew what happened. It wasn't the first time. But right there, seeing her half-naked, crying and bruised, I felt so sorry for her.

Why does she keep doing this stuff? I wondered. It was like a game to her.

I let her hug me. She squeezed me with such force it was hard to breathe. And she got her eye makeup all over my pajama top. I ran my hand down her long, ebony hair until her sobs turned to tiny rhythmic snores. Then I left her sleeping on the living room floor and went back to my bed.

I called Grandpa at work the next day. "Mom is sick," I told him. After a long silence, he told me to pack as much as we could into our knapsacks. Then he came over while Mom was still sleeping and took Cam and me back to their house for another two-week vacation.

Again nobody said anything to her or even asked Cam or me what happened. The only thing I trusted was that something was making my mom do these weird things. And not one person would help her...or us. My conclusion was that people didn't know how sick she really was, so they didn't know how to help her. But because they didn't want to hear about it, Cam and I kept going between a life with Mom and a life with my grandparents until someone did want to hear about it.

After staying at my grandparents' house that last time after mom's fight with Muriel, our family wouldn't come and save Cam and me anymore. I figured they thought the only way to "fix" my mom was to make her take responsibility – for herself...for us. We kept her going and gave her a reason to want to do better. But whatever kept making Mom so crazy-happy one day then so sad the next came more often, stayed longer, and got stronger with each visit. And it soon hurt Cam and me in other ways.

Mom and Lyle partied quite often with a couple who had two children close to our ages. The couple's son, Chris, was a little older than I. I found it creepy that a kid who was only about eight years old was so touchy/feely. Most boys I knew weren't even interested in girls yet. They just wanted to roughhouse and play sports. But those of us who grew up with hippie parents – the ones who believed in the "Free Love" theory of the Sixties – were more knowledgeable and curious about sex than other children were.

Now, I wasn't naïve about sex – Mom didn't hide her behavior or close her door often. Unfortunately, I knew more than I should have for my age. And I didn't really want to know. Something about it disgusted me...scared me. In our house,

sex was a thing to use for control...to manipu-
late. It was nothing like how they made it seem
on the soaps or movies or those romance books.

One evening, after a delectable barbecue
dinner of steak, baked potatoes and salads – and
many, many drinks – Chris' parents, Lyle and
Mom sat around the piano and sang while Chris
lured me upstairs to my bedroom to "teach me
about something."

I had a feeling when he said we had to go
into my closet that the lesson would be something a bit more than I was comfortable with.
"Can't you just show me out here?" I asked.

Chris clicked his tongue. "No, Stupid. It's
private." Then he pulled me into the closet and
maneuvered the door shut.

My bedroom light peeked under the door
as Chris told me to take my pants and underwear off.

"Forget it!" I said, folding my arms. "I don't
want to take my stuff off."

"Don't worry." Chris said. "I'll take mine off,
too."

That wasn't very reassuring. Chris took off his
clothes, then tugged at mine. He wanted to
show me how to have sex, but his version of it
wasn't what I'd seen in my mother's room when
Lyle slept over.

We sat on the floor of the closet with our legs
straight out. Then he put his hand between my
legs and guided mine between his. That was it,
but it grossed me out. And it happened every
time Chris and his parents visited. He never got

caught, but I became so upset before they came over, Mom finally asked about it.

"What's wrong with you, Tam?" she asked while putting on her mascara. "I thought you liked playing with Chris. He's always so excited to come over and see you guys."

Yeah, I'll just bet he is, I thought. I looked down, tears stinging my eyes. I didn't think I could tell her. I was too ashamed.

"I don't like him," I said. "He touches me, Mom. And he makes me touch him. Every time they come over here. I don't like it, and I don't like him."

All those *Degrassi Junior High* episodes I had seen with the message to "Tell Someone" all seemed to make everything okay in the end. I thought I'd be hugged and told that everything would be taken care of. I thought Mom would be angry with Chris and his parents and demand justice.

Well, she was angry – but not at Chris.

"You're making this up, aren't you?" Mom said, glaring down at me. "You don't want to share me with anyone else, so you're making up stories to have me all to yourself. Unless you can come up with an honest, logical reason for them not to come here anymore, they'll continue to. If you don't like that, go live with Grandma."

I couldn't believe it. I told her what happened and even described the huge, leaf-shaped birthmark on his lower abdomen, but she refused to believe me. They continued coming over, and Chris kept doing it. That is, until he'd somehow given me an infection and I had to go to the doctor. The doctor wrote it off as a bladder infection, but I guess Mom finally believed me because we never saw Chris or his family again. We never talked about what happened with Chris again, either. The doctor gave me a few days' prescription for a thick, uncomfortable cream that smelled like aspirin. That made the problem disappear, at least physically.

After the incidents with Muriel and Chris, we moved into a condo-style apartment we couldn't afford. Lyle moved with us – I guess that's what you'd call it. His trucking jobs got longer and longer but he kept all of his stuff at our place. He had the coolest stereo speakers that flashed and flickered blue, purple, green and other colors to the beat of the songs. He also had a waterbed and other fun stuff. He even liked playing games and sports with us and taught us how to play Blackjack and Poker. Once in a while, though, when someone brought up marriage – either Mom or her friends – he'd shut right up and chug a few beers.

This was not a love-in approved by my grandparents, and we didn't see them much while Mom and Lyle shacked up. Cam and I still went to church, but Mom didn't want to go to my grandparents' house for Christmas Eve that year. She said it "wasn't worth the fights." But the three of us ended up going over for Christmas Day and stayed overnight. Lyle stayed at home. When we got back home the next day, our apartment had been cleaned out. All of Lyle's stuff – and some of Mom's – was gone. A "Dear Jane" letter lay on Mom's piano bench.

There was no delusion that Lyle was ever going to marry Mom, but they had fun. I think he just had enough of her wild mood swings and never-ending partying, and was tired of being the emotional punching bag for the stuff going on between Mom and my grandparents. Even though Mom had a lot of students, she was only able to afford the rent in the condo for a few more months. Then we had to move again.

We moved several times during my childhood. Our moves usually followed events similar to what happened with Muriel. And the places she chose were far beyond her financial capacity, so we ended up moving again after only a few months. These moves were difficult for Cam and me because we never felt like we could settle down anywhere. After our move into the condo, we kept some of our stuff packed because we knew another move loomed around the corner.

Cam and I didn't care if we lived somewhere with a pool, tennis courts, or game room. We just wanted our own rooms where we could safely take out all of our stuff and put it away permanently.

Fortunately, we were always able to get back into the townhouse project we first stayed in. And the last time we moved back there, after Lyle left us, we kept the same townhouse for several years. Thank God, because we were starved for some sort of stability. The first couple of weeks after we'd moved back into the townhouse, I woke up with Cam either curled up at the bottom of my bed or laying on the floor beside it. At first, I didn't mind. Cam often came into my room when Mom had parties or things were too loud or he had nightmares. But after two weeks, sharing my room with my little brother was getting annoying.

"Cam, go to your own room," I finally said. "You have your own room with your own bed. Get out!"

Cam started crying. "But I can't find Doggie, and I like my room. What if I get used to it and we leave again?"

I sighed. I got out of bed, grabbed his hand and led him back into his room. It was smaller than mine, but he didn't have much stuff. When I pushed his door wider, I saw all his boxes were still sealed up. Mom had made his bed but left it up to him to unpack his stuff. I rolled my eyes.

I found the box marked, "Bed stuffies and shelf toys," ripped it open and pulled out Doggie – his favorite bright yellow dog. It had a zippered pouch on its tummy where you could store pajamas and other secret stuff. Doggie felt stuffed so I searched inside and found his favorite blankie, too. "Cam, why didn't you open up your things? See? I found Doggie and Blankie."

He sniffed and wiped his nose on his pajama sleeve. "Dunno. Guess I just wanted to be ready for the next time we have to go."

My eyes stung. I gave him his stuff, got him into his bed, then went to my own room. Part of me understood what he was saying. In the darkness of my own room, I could still make out the ugly bright pink and purple flowered wallpaper. I hated that wallpaper but didn't want to ask to take it down. What was the point of making my room the way I liked it if we were going to leave in a few months?

Cam and I needed that feeling of stability... unfortunately it wasn't going to come anytime soon.

Chapter Three

The Diary

Betrayal can only happen if you love.
~ John LeCarre (1931—)

When I was young, my favorite time of year had to be Christmas. We spent every Christmas at my grandparents' house, with the exception of one, when Mom and my grandparents were fighting about Lyle. My mom still drank on Christmas. Sometimes too much. Okay, oftentimes, too much. But for a couple of days of the year we felt like a real family.

We decorated my grandparents' tree on Christmas Eve. Grandpa made a fire while Bing Crosby sang "White Christmas." The house smelled like cookies, turkey and other goodies. Cam and I always bet who could steal the most After Eight chocolates from Grandma's stash before she noticed. Most important though were all the hugs and "I love you's" that made me feel so good. These happy memories were what I would reminisce about years later, when Christmas became a darker time.

The Christmas I was nine, it seemed important to Mom that we start all over (again). After Lyle left us, she wasn't able to lift herself out of her sadness for a month. She stayed in bed most of the time, crying. She didn't eat or exercise or watch *All My Children* – she just cried. Somehow she was able to hold it together enough to teach her piano students, but then she went back to bed or just sat on the couch staring at the television. This was even worse because she didn't seem to hear us or notice anything going on around her. We had to get right in her face and scream at her to get her attention, "Mom! Can we have a snack?" I had a stomach ache every day – like a pointy rock jabbing me with worry.

Cam and I tried everything to bring our mother out, but nothing seemed to work. I was terrified to fall asleep before she did, because I was afraid she wouldn't be there when I woke up. I had nightmares of her dying, or leaving us to find Lyle. Then, just as suddenly as the sadness overtook her, it disappeared again. Like every other time, something sparked in her and she seemed to get a renewed energy for life again.

On Christmas Eve that year, she came into Grandma's living room – where the rest of us were watching *How The Grinch Stole Christmas* – dressed up in her cheery, red satin pantsuit. She'd cut her hair into a long shag and gotten some waves and highlights put in. She even put makeup on. She looked so beautiful – better than I'd seen her in so long.

"Everyone will be here soon," Grandma said to Mom. "Why don't you get the kids into their good clothes?"

Mom looked down at us wearing our jeans and sweaters and winked. "They're dressed fine for now. We're going out for a couple of hours, and we'll change when we come back, right guys?"

We looked at each other, then nodded. Mom disappeared into the den. Grandma folded her arms over her chest. "What do you mean you're going out? I told you that everyone was going to be here by seven o'clock. And what about church?"

Grandma always had a few friends over on Christmas Eve before we went to the late church service at eleven. Mom didn't like Grandma's parties. She was expected to go around and talk to everyone, serving the dainties. Later Grandma would ask her to sing and play the piano. I understood why she didn't like the waitressing part – I never liked that either. That year, I was old enough to serve anything that wouldn't stain. But Mom seemed to cheer up when she played and sang. And when I got older, we played duets. I hated dressing up – I just wasn't a "girlie girl" like Grandma thought girls should be – but I never minded the piano playing and singing. It made my grandparents so happy.

Mom came back into the room with a tumbler glass filled with a milky drink. She stood next to me. The smell of rum was so strong, I coughed. "We'll be back in an hour-and-a-half, Mom – if that," my mom said to Grandma. "I just have presents to drop off to a few friends." She tipped her glass up and sucked back a huge swig of her Christmas nog.

Grandma glared. "Do you really think you should be drinking that before going out on the road?"

Mom looked between Grandma and us. Butterflies fluttered in my stomach. Mom's cheeks crimsoned. She took another big gulp and put the glass back down, with a bit too much force, shaking the dining room table and all the sterling silver trays filled with food and Christmas dainties like little shortbread cookies, tiny gingersnaps and butter tarts. Then she said, "Kids? Get your stuff on."

Mom and Grandma stared at each other for what felt like hours. I nudged Cam and we went down the hall to get our coats and boots. I heard loud whispering so I made sure we took our time getting ready, then I dragged Cam through the kitchen door to avoid going past my mom and grandmother. I had no idea what they were saying, but Mom's eyes were teary.

She put on a little smile while she zipped up her black leather high-heeled boots and slipped on her long, black-and-red-checkered coat. "Grandma needs some help with her party, so we'll go visit a few people, give them their presents, and come right back, okay guys?"

"Aw, but I really wanted to play with Sarah."
I whined, then quickly shut up. Mom closed her
eyes and sighed, pulling on her black leather
gloves. "I know, honey. But we have to come
back quick – I promised Grandma. Maybe we
can try meeting up with Sarah and her mom
sometime over the holidays."

So we played Santa to Mom's friends, returned
as server/entertainers for Grandma's party, went
to the candle lighting service at church, then
were sent to bed.

Mom's older brother, who lived in Toronto and
only came in a couple of times a year, was there.
On Christmas morning, Mom and Uncle Rick
looked like they were sick or something. Kind of
like how my mom looked the morning after
she'd been up all night partying. I dismissed that
thought because I was sure my grandmother
wouldn't have tolerated that stuff in her house.
I realized later they'd been up all night playing
Santa and putting our toys together. I remember
waking up, hearing "Santa," aka Grandpa, cursing
about the instructions for my Barbie Motor Home.

We opened our stockings and all of our gifts
under the tree. While Grandma started our traditional Christmas brunch of eggs, bacon, toast
with homemade strawberry jam, and good strong
coffee, Mom surprised Cam and me with our grand
finale gift.

Mom told us to sit down because she had a
huge surprise for us. Cam and I sat together in
Grandpa's green velvet barrel chair and waited
for our big gift. We closed our eyes, as instructed,

and when we opened them, each of us had a small folder with flight itinerary and general information about Disneyworld. We both sat there staring at the folders in our hands with frowns on our faces. I was so shocked, I couldn't think of anything to say. And Cam was confused because he expected a "Big Present" to be in a much bigger box.

Mom seemed hurt by our reactions. I think she expected us to jump up, run around screaming or, at the very least, wrap our arms around her and thank her. But we didn't.

She pointed to the agenda on my folder. "We're going to Disneyworld, see? For Spring Break. Isn't that great?"

I tried smiling. I tried looking excited. But the only thought in my head was, *No way am I going somewhere that far away with just you.*

"Thank you," I mumbled. Mom rolled her eyes and left the living room.

"Where's the big gift?" Cam asked.

I left everyone else laughing at Cam's unintentional joke and hunted Mom down in the basement. She was in the laundry room putting a load of towels in the dryer. Guilt flooded over me. I stood in the shadows watching her for a minute before I spoke to her. Sometimes I did that. I watched her when she didn't know I was there. She looked so normal. For just one moment I saw her the same way strangers did and wished I didn't see her the way I did.

"Mom," I finally said. "I'm sorry. It just doesn't seem real yet, that's all. We'll be more excited when it's closer to the time we go."

She brightened and pulled me into her chest, kissing the top of my head. "It'll be great. You'll see."

"Yeah. Great."

I squeezed my eyes shut and prayed that she was right.

Spring Break came so fast – faster than I wanted it to. Actually, aside from Cam and me being exposed to chicken pox before we left on our trip – and breaking out in spots the day before we came back – and Mom having a bronchitis attack, things went fairly well on our trip for the first few days.

We all had great fun eating out, going to the theme park, and swimming in the hotel pool. But after a few days, I could tell Mom was either bored or restless, because she introduced herself to people – mostly men – at the hotel pool. She wasn't able to sit still, and chewed her fingernails down to the quick. The excited butterflies that soared in my belly when our plane touched down in Florida sank one by one. I hoped she'd hold it together. It was only for a week, right? But signs of another crash were lined up when, on only the third night into our trip, I woke up in the hotel room without our mother there.

I curled into a ball on my side, tears running down my face into my pillow. It just wasn't enough for her. We weren't enough for her. As the air conditioner whirred in the background and faceless conversation drifted up from poolside, fear flooded over me. There we were in another country with no Grandma and Grandpa within walking distance, and our mother was absent. What if she took off for good this time? How would we get back home?

I rolled over onto my back and pulled the covers up. I should have known when she drank too much on the plane and freaked out because the pressure in her ears wouldn't equalize with altitude changes that we were in trouble. But I gave her the benefit of the doubt.

I lay on the king-sized bed I shared with Cam. My knuckles turned white as I gripped the sheets under my chin. After what seemed like hours, I heard keys jingling. After some fumbling they dropped to the floor.

Giggles.

A male voice offered assistance.

A male voice?

A shot of adrenaline exploded from my sto-mach out to my extremities making my fingers and toes tingle. My heart pounded. Cam and I were trapped. I had an idea what was about to happen and there was no way I wanted to be a witness to it. (Let's just say when Mom finally got around to giving me "the talk" a couple of years later, I already knew more than a kid my age needed to.) Our room had a small closet, two king-sized beds, a desk with a television, a bathroom and a little table with a couple of chairs. And with only one door to go in or out, I had no way to sneak us out. What were we supposed to do? Hide in the closet? I shut my eyes and pretended I was asleep.

After several minutes of key fumbling and giggling, they got the door open. The air conditioner wafted the smell of cheap wine and cigarettes around the room. Mom turned on the television, both for background noise and ambience since she didn't want to wake us up. I wondered if Cam was awake. As if on cue, he cuddled into my side.

What followed was a lot of gross, loud slurpy kissing – the kind of kissing they do in the soap operas where it's overacted – and some heavy breathing and moaning. I squinted my eyes open just a crack to see where they were, hoping to find my opportunity to escape. They weren't on the bed but on the floor beside the table and chairs. I sniffed softly and squished my eyes closed again.

Please just let it be over with fast, I prayed.

Ten minutes of grunted wrestling, then the guy got up, said, "See ya by the pool," and left. Mom flopped down on her own king-sized bed and, after a few minutes, snored. I rolled over onto my stomach and cried. I was sad, ashamed, and so disappointed. I just didn't understand how someone so smart kept doing such stupid things.

I realized that somehow, I had to get my mother the help she needed. Even if I was the only one who tried.

When we returned from Orlando, Cam and I were sick with chicken pox for over two weeks. With so much time on my hands while in quarantine, I made a plan to figure out how to help my mom – the first of many plans. Before our trip, I'd gone into her writing desk, forbidden to us, to steal an envelope, and had made a fantastic, yet frightening, discovery: Mom's diaries.

There were two of them. One was sky-blue leather with a pretty – but useless – gold lock, to ward off snoopers. The other was white with gold-tipped pages and no lock. I was shocked she left them so easily accessible. Girls are usually much more protective of their precious secrets. It was as though a part of her wanted someone to read them.

I decided to accept the invitation.

My plan was simple: the first time she left us alone in the house, I would read as much as I could from one and put it back exactly the way she'd placed it. I knew it was wrong – a sin among women – but I was sure that the secret behind my mother's behavior was in those books of memories, and I had to read them. If there was something – anything – I could do to end this suffering for everyone, especially her, I needed to try.

I got my chance one afternoon when she went over to a neighbor's place. When I heard the door slam shut, I sprinted to her room and looked out the window to confirm her departure.

I yanked down the door of the writing desk and stared at the diaries. My arms hung at my sides like lead. I don't think I was afraid to get caught. At that point I really didn't care. I was more afraid of what I might read.

What if the diaries did have all the answers? Was I really ready to read about them? Did I want to know my mother that well? Or, worse still, what if there were no answers?

I didn't care. I needed to try.

I grabbed the blue book and hustled back to my room. My heart pounded as I popped the lock and cracked opened the faux-leather cover. I wasn't prepared for the words on the pages.

Mom had her own version of what things were like for her growing up. She told Cam and me many stories about her childhood, about our grandparents, about my dad and his family, even about her personal morals and ethics. But in her diary, she told an entirely different version of those stories.

See, a person doesn't lie to their diary – at least I never did. It's the one place I could vent, speak my mind, lighten my heart, reveal my skeletons, and trust that I wouldn't be judged. I was honest with my journal because I never thought anyone else would read it – or care, if they did. As I read her diary a deep sadness swept over me because I realized that the stories she'd told us from when she was a teen-ager to when she had me weren't necessarily lies, but more the way she wished her life could have been.

There were things she'd told us that I questioned but never challenged because I had no proof, but on that day, I finally did. I learned how and why I was conceived, her true feelings for my dad, how she was talked out of an abortion, and even sent off to a private school in an attempt to "fix her." There were pages and pages of her talking about being so sad that she wanted to die but didn't have the courage to take action. Then there were pages and pages about the impulsive things she did, like running away with some guy, or drinking and taking drugs, or having sex when she was fifteen:

Well he and I did "it" again. In the basement this time with Mom and Dad upstairs. It wasn't so bad this time. Had to drink and took a few aspirins. Maybe he'll help me get out of here. They don't care anyway. If it doesn't work this time, I'll just kill myself.

That's what most of her entries were like. She seemed to hate herself so much. A heaviness filled my heart. The way she talked about her life and herself when she was drunk or really sad – was just like in her diary. I couldn't understand how someone could be that unhappy but nobody seemed to notice. Or did they?

I didn't care that she lied about being a virgin when she met my dad. I didn't care that she lied about getting pregnant with me on purpose to get away from my grandparents. I didn't care that she wanted an abortion and my godmother talked her into keeping me. I didn't even care that she said she hated me many times in those pages – it wasn't like she never said it to my face. But nobody should feel that way so much or so often.

I wanted to put the book down. I didn't want or need to read anymore. I had more answers than I needed, but I couldn't stop. Her entries seemed scattered at times. Sometimes she was self-loathing and destructive; other times way too confident – almost cocky. It was confusing to read. I couldn't imagine what it must have been like to be in her mind. How was I supposed to help a person like that?

Cam often wondered why our mother and I never got along, why she abused me so much when she drank and why she was so apologetic later. I believed that she loved me but also hated me. There was a dark part of her that resented me for coming into her world and ruining her free spirit. The part that loved me felt guilty about these resentful feelings and tried to make up for it.

Just as I was about to put the book back into her desk, Mom opened my door. I froze.

"Hey, Tam, what...?" She spied the blue book in my hands. Her face changed. The hatred I saw in her eyes when she drank was there. "You really are a true bitch, you know that? Who the hell do you think you are?"

She tried snatching the diary out of my hands but I gripped it as hard as I could. I forced myself to stare right into her green eyes.

"I know everything, Mom. And I'm not covering for you anymore. I'm going to make sure you can't hide anything from anyone. You need help, and if you don't get it, I'm taking Cam and getting out of here."

Whack! She hit my head with the lock side of the book and knocked me sideways with a soft landing on my bed. I refused to cry in front of her.

"Fuck you, Tami," she said through gritted teeth, tears flooding her eyes. She slammed my door behind her.

I held my head and cried. There was an unspoken challenge between my mother and me that day which lasted until she died. I tried as hard as I could to expose the evil thing inside of her that was trying to take her away from us, and she tried as hard as she could to prove me wrong. I had the advantage though. I knew the truth and was willing to talk about it.

I just needed to make other people see it and do the same.

Chapter Four

Last Chance

Death is not the greatest loss in life.
The greatest loss is what dies inside
us while we live.
~ Norman Cousins (1912-1990)

For the next few months, the atmosphere in our house was tense. Mom jumped on every opportunity to start a fight with me. I felt like a private in the military. I had to be on my toes in case a test or inspection popped up: Bed made? Clothes put away? Room tidy? And God forbid I wasn't ready!

I suppose I deserved it. I knew what it was like to have my privacy invaded. Mom was so paranoid that Cam and I were up to something, she listened in on our telephone conversations, invited herself to hang out with us and our friends – and she read my diary, too.

Admittedly, half of the tension stemmed from my own anger. I was angry that I didn't understand her illness or know how to help. And angry at her unpredictable behavior, at our family and her friends who saw everything but did nothing, and at myself for staying silent. I felt trapped – helpless.

Mom and I seemed to struggle with similar feelings, and we both fought the same unseen assailant – her illness. The only difference was that I wanted to square off with it and she wouldn't acknowledge it. Our refusal to see each other's side caused enormous eruptions.

At breakfast one morning, Mom primped and fussed in front of the mirror while Cam and I tried to force down a bowl of gray, lumpy, half-cooked oatmeal. She had an interview, and we were taking too long to eat breakfast.

"C'mon, you guys, I have to be there in fifteen minutes," she said while plucking her eyebrows. "What's taking you so long?"

Poor Cam tried his best to shovel it in. He was never the fastest eater at the best of times or the best of meals. Grandma used to tell him he was "slower than molasses in January." I think he did it on purpose, as his own way of rebelling.

"Take it easy, Mom. He's doing his best."

"And what's wrong with your breakfast? It's exactly the same as his."

I shrugged. "Not hungry, I guess."

The truth was I didn't feel well. I'd been up all the night before. I trained myself to wake up at the slightest noise so I'd always know what went on in our house. I knew when my mom left, or if anyone showed up at our house, and I knew when she arrived home.

Mom threw her hairbrush in front of my bowl. "Just eat." She stood beside me, waiting for me to spoon some food in.

"No," I said.

"Excuse me?"

"I said no."

"I heard what you said, Tam."

"Then why did you ask what I said?"

She slammed her hand down on the table. My spoon rattled against my bowl. "Don't push me, Little Girl. Not today."

I looked up at her without expression. She had way too much eye makeup on. "I'm not hungry, Mom. I'll just take an apple for recess."

"No, you won't," she said. "You'll eat your breakfast."

My eyes narrowed. "Make me."

Whack!

She slapped me with the back of her hand. My nose popped and poured blood. Cam shoved huge spoonfuls of oatmeal into his mouth. I ran from the table with my hand filling with blood, footsteps thundering behind me.

I sat on the bathroom floor, reaching for Kleenex after Kleenex, trying to stop the geyser pouring out of my nose. Blood saturated one sheet before I could reach for another. Mom stood in the doorway for a few seconds just staring at me. Then she rushed to the sink and soaked a washcloth with cold water.

"Here, let's put this on your nose," she said.

I pushed her hand away. "Get away from me."

She clicked her tongue and rolled her eyes. "You're fine. It's just a nosebleed. It was an accident."

She'd spanked me before. Once she broke a wooden spoon on my bum because Cam and I drew on our bedroom wall with crayons. When we were younger, though, she was always more of a yeller than a hitter. That day it was different. The way she hit me was from pure anger.

I threw the washcloth at her. It left a wet mark on the front of her blue satiny blouse. She screeched. "Look what you did!" She smacked the back of my head to emphasize each word. Blood droplets splattered on the tiles and my clothes.

"Oh God, Tam. I...I have to change. Clean up, okay? I'll drive you guys to school on the way to my interview. Maybe we'll go somewhere nice for supper. Sound good?"

I didn't answer her. After fifteen more minutes, my nose finally stopped bleeding. As I cleaned the floor, Cam walked in. He stared at me with innocence I wished I still had.

"You should'a just eaten the oatmeal, Tam," he said, shoving his hands into his pockets. "Why do you do that stuff when you know what'll happen?"

I pulled his left hand out of his pocket and tugged him downstairs. Mom waited for us in the car. She was late for her interview. In the rush to clean the bathroom, I'd forgotten to change my clothes. It was okay though because not one person at school asked me why I had blood on my clothes.

As I walked home from school I thought about how good our mother could be. When I'd had trouble at school with bullies, she marched right into the principal's office and demanded justice for me. When I had nightmares, if she was there, she rushed in to ease me through them. I even remember times where she starved herself so Cam and I had enough to eat. So, *why*, I wondered, *why did she act like she did earlier that morning if she loved us so much?*

While I shuffled up the sidewalk, I prayed that I hadn't ruined Mom's chances at her interview. As the screen door slammed behind me, she stuck her head around the corner from the living room and said, "Come on in, Sunshine. I have good news."

She had amnesia about the morning.

Fine with me.

When I got into the living room, Cam was already there. Mom had brought home some new hockey cards for him which he gleefully browsed through. His cheeks were stuffed with the pink bubble gum that came tucked into the card packages. I laughed at him. I couldn't help it – he looked like a chipmunk.

He gave me a goofy smile and pink spit dribbled out of the side of his mouth. A smile spread across my face. I burst into laughter. Tears streamed down my cheeks. Mom turned around to see what was so funny. Cam laughed so hard he accidentally spit the enormous pink wad out onto the carpet. That sent Mom into laughing hysterics.

For a brief moment, things seemed so normal. Those were times I clung to. They gave me hope for the possibility of change. I sniffed, cringing because my nose was still swollen and tender, then wiped my eyes.

Mom let out one more snort. "Wow. Anyway, I was telling Cam just before you came in that we should go to Grapes for dinner. Would you like that? Anything you want."

"Really?" I said. "Can we afford it?"

She ran her fingers through her long black hair, flipping the ends up so she could pick off a few split ends. "Well, I didn't get the job. But I did sign on four new students! That makes 35 now. I think we'll be okay. We should be doing this sort of thing more often – at least once a week. Just the three of us. Besides, we also have something special to celebrate."

I'd almost forgotten that it was my tenth birthday. I worried about how hard she tried to assure me everything was okay. But I figured, *Why cut her down when she tried?*

"Sounds great!" I remembered my clothes. "Just let me change, okay?"

Mom disappeared into the kitchen. "Go ahead, Birthday Girl. We'll have about an hour anyway. I'll call for a reservation."

I ran up the stairs. I was so excited! It would be the first time in a long time that we were going out for supper to a place where our meals wouldn't come with a big yellow "M" on the wrappers.

Just the three of us.

My heart filled with hope. Maybe things would be different now. Maybe we just needed to hit a skid to make us realize how much we needed to have time to bond again.

I showered, got into my best jeans and t-shirt, and brushed my hair. I ran back downstairs to see Cam re-organizing his hockey cards in front of *Get Smart* on the television. My smile disappeared when I saw Mom with a glass of wine – filled to the brim – in her hand. My heart sank.

But then I figured, *Oh well.* Grandpa always had a drink when he came home from work – before he retired. *Things would be fine,* I thought. *She wouldn't let anything bad happen today. Not on my birthday. One drink wouldn't hurt.*

She lit up a cigarette then asked, "Would you like some?"

I was confused. "I don't smoke. That's disgusting."

Mom laughed, blowing smoke out of the side of her mouth. "Not the cigarette, Silly. Would you like your own little glass of wine? It's okay if you do. It's Mateus."

"Uhm...no thanks," I said. "I'll just have Coke at the restaurant."

That was new. She'd never asked if I wanted my own glass of something before. I mean, Cam and I snuck tastes of beer or whatever was around from the bottles or glasses at her parties, but that was it.

She shrugged. "Okay. What about you, Cam? Would you like some wine?"

Cam looked up at her, then at me. I didn't give him the chance to answer. "Mom, he's only seven. Besides, he doesn't like wine."

"It's okay, Tam." Cam smiled.

"No, it isn't, Cam." I looked right into his eyes. His smile faded.

Mom chugged the rose liquid like it was icy cold water on a hot summer day. "Fine with me. Let's go, guys. This'll be fun."

I figured one glass of wine wouldn't affect her driving as long as she didn't have any more. I eased as we talked about what we planned to order. Mom said we could have anything we wanted on the menu. To make it fun, she made a rule we had to order something we'd never tried before.

We were seated in a booth by the window near the back of the restaurant. In those days, there were no "Smoking" or "Nonsmoking" sections. I guess if you didn't want to inhale other people's smoke you simply asked to be moved.

As we reviewed the menus, our waiter came to introduce himself. "Good evening folks, I'm Cam. I'll be your waiter for this evening. Can I get you anything from the bar?"

Cam the Waiter looked like one of those guys from California. He had unkempt sun-streaked blonde hair that fluttered around his shoulders. His skin was bronzed and made his blue eyes glow. And his teeth were unnaturally white – they reminded me of little squares of Chiclets gum. Mom liked him, though. Her right eyebrow rose when she looked at him. I slumped back in the booth, folding my arms over my chest.

"Isn't that cool?" she said. "His name is Cam, too?"

Giggles.

Yuck. I rolled my eyes. "Yeah. What are the odds, finding another guy named Cam?"

She shot me a "shut-up" look, then took a cigarette out and put it between her pursed lips. Waiter Cam whipped out a mini bright yellow lighter from his shirt pocket – the buttons undone to his pecs, of course – and sparked it in front of Mom's face. She looked at him from the corner of her eye, cupping her hand over his, and brought it to her cigarette.

Oh geez. I wanted Waiter Cam to go away.

Mom puffed smoke out while she spoke. "Well, Cam, I'd like a Rusty Nail. It's my daughter's tenth birthday today, and I'm sure she'd love a Shirley Temple. Wouldn't ya, Honey?"

I didn't want a stupid baby drink. "I'll have a Coke, please. No ice."

"Well, happy birthday!" said Waiter Cam. "I'll bring your drinks right away."

Two Rusty Nails and a carafe-and-a-half of wine later, my birthday dinner turned into a total disaster and a scene way too mature for kids. Several other staff members hung out at our table, including the manager, and Waiter Cam spent more time at our table than anyone else's. In fact, he sat at our booth when he got off his shift. But not before getting everyone around our table – including the few people still left in the restaurant – to sing "Happy Birthday" to me. I sat through the awful singing then shoved my plate in front of my brother. There was nothing worse than being sung to, off key and over-the-top loud, by a bunch of strangers.

When Mom and Waiter Cam started ordering double Rusty Nails, I decided Cam and I needed to make our escape. I leaned over to Cam, who'd been enjoying my free birthday cake, and said, "C'mon. We're outta here."

He looked at our mother and nodded.

"She'll come home later, Cam," I said, stuffing his arms into his jacket sleeves. "I promise."

I grabbed Mom's purse, took out her key ring, then slid out of the booth with Cam's hand in mine.

She stopped mid-laugh. "Where ya goin'? Aren't you having fun?"

"Not anymore." I said.

The table went silent. Everyone looked at Mom. She cleared her throat, "Cam here can sing and play guitar."

I shook my head. "Great. Our Cam is tired and I'm taking him home. I have the keys."

She took a long drag from her cigarette and poked the tips of her fingers into her hair. Waiter Cam tried smoothing things over. He knelt down so we were at eye level. His breath was sour. "Hey, look. If you stick around a bit longer, I can give you all a drive home. Would that be okay?"

"No, it wouldn't be okay, Cam," I said. "My brother and I are walking. Thanks for the dinner, Mom."

I supposed I'd said something funny because laughter exploded as we walked away from the table. I turned to see our mother sitting in

Waiter Cam's lap with her arms wrapped around his neck. My eyes burned with tears.

Fortunately, we only lived about three blocks from the restaurant – that's why we'd always chosen it. It was dark, but our area was well lit and active, so I knew we were safe. I'd stopped calling Grandpa when things like that happened. The result would have been the same: he'd get us, we'd stay with them a couple of nights then we'd go right back to Mom. Why bother upsetting them?

I put Cam in his bed, got into my pajamas, then listened.

Silence.

There was no way I was going to fall asleep until I knew Mom was back home. As mad as I was at her, I also worried. When she got really drunk, it was as if she lost all care about what happened to herself or us. I tried stopping the drinks from coming. I'd even begged Waiter Cam not to bring her any more.

I wondered if something happened at her interview that she didn't tell us about. The more I thought about how I'd just left her at the res-taurant, the guiltier I felt. Just as I was about to throw my clothes back on and run back to get her, I heard the front door open.

I got out of bed and heard male mumblings as I got to the top of the stairs. My heart raced. My hands were ice cold. I leaned over the wall to see Waiter Cam helping Mom walk to the base-ment door.

At least she came home. But I didn't fall asleep until I heard the front door shut again, heard his car drive away, then heard Mom go up to her room. As I drifted off, I heard her muffled sniffles.

Happy birthday to me.

We missed church the next morning. Grandma didn't even call to find out where we were. Cam and I sat on the floor watching cartoons in our pajamas with a cookie jar full of chocolate chip cookies between us. The doorbell rang. Forgetting I was still in my pajamas and, I'm sure, with chocolate all over my face, I answered the door to see a girl about my age.

"Hi there," she said. "I'm here for my piano lesson. I'm new and Janet said I could come today."

I knew there was no way our mother was in any shape to teach. If she'd come down hung over, that would have been the first and last lesson for her new student.

"Oh, geez," I said, crossing my arms over my stomach. "My mom is real sick. We went out last night for dinner and she ate something bad, I think. The doctor came over and everything! I'm sorry I didn't call you, but I didn't know she had a new student. Can you call my mom tomorrow and arrange another lesson? I'm sure she'll make extra time."

"Yeah, sure," she said. "I'll tell my mom. Thanks. It's okay – it'll give me a chance to practice a bit more before I play for her. I hear she's pretty good."

It was nice to know that people out there still appreciated her musical abilities. "Yeah. She's really good – one of the best."

An hour after the girl left, the phone rang. I wasn't sure whether to answer it in case it was my grandparents. It was my Uncle Craig. He didn't sound happy. "Hey, Tam. Missed you guys in church this morning. So, where's your Mom? She okay?"

Great. I had to lie again – to my uncle of all people. "Yeah. She's just sick."

He forced a chuckle. "Sick, huh? Where is she, Tammer?"

"She's upstairs, sleeping," I said.

His voice didn't sound as convinced as Mom's new student's did. "I'm coming over there." He hung up without saying goodbye.

I grabbed a cookie out of Cam's hand, just before he put it in his mouth, and threw it back into the cookie jar.

"Hey! That's mine!" he said.

I turned off the television. "Forget about that! Uncle Craig is coming over. Quick! Get dressed and wash your face."

Cam and I scrambled. Just as we got back downstairs, Uncle Craig stormed into our town-house. Uncle Craig is six-foot-four, so we made sure to move if we were in his path. His face was stern, his walk was hurried, and his cheeks were flushed.

"Where's your Mom?" he asked, snapping his gum.

I nodded upstairs. He stomped up the stairs three at a time – impressive in flip-flops – and barged into her room. We heard the conversation from downstairs.

"Janet? Janet? Wake up. You reek like booze."

She groaned in response.

"Look, I know I said I wouldn't give you any money, but I sent you these new students to help you out and then you go out and get loaded. I got a call from my friend saying she hoped you recovered from your food poisoning. Food poisoning my ass! Janet!"

Still no response.

"Don't ask me for anything again," Uncle Craig said. "I won't help you when you do this crap."

He slammed Mom's bedroom door then stomped back down the stairs. We ran to the couch. Uncle Craig stood with his hands on his hips staring at us. He sighed. "Get your shoes on. We'll go to the zoo."

God Bless Uncle Craig.

Chapter Five

From Serenity to Insanity

On the second day, God created angels, with their natural propensity to good. Later He made beasts with their animal desires. But God was pleased with neither. So He fashioned man, a combination of angel and beast, free to follow good or evil.

~ Midrash Semak

When Mom was a little girl, my grandfather bought a piece of land at West Hawk Lake in Lake of the Woods, Ontario. He built a modest cabin hugged into the hillside by towering pine trees. It was my mother's sanctuary.

Our driveway was at the bottom of a large hill marked by a simple sign, "Batty – Lot 29" (later marked as "Nicol's Quarters" after Mom remarried).

The driveway itself was made of broken dark granite, with tufts of green weeds creeping out here and there. The backyard was mostly sand after years of cars coming and going, wearing the grass away. A massive birch stood proudly in the middle of the yard, much to the frustration of anyone who tried parking back there. Bark hung off the gnarled trunk in black and white curls.

A three-foot stone wall that Grandpa made himself wound the length of the driveway and burst with color and scent all summer long. Grandpa kept the hollowed-out top filled with various lilies, pansies and wildflowers. After my grandparents stopped visiting the cabin, our mother filled it with vegetables.

The best time of day was dusk, when the action on the water settled and the loons bellowed their throaty night song. If there was no wind, the water was like glass and we could see the jagged rocky bottom. I used to close my eyes and drink in the atmosphere. The tiny ripples kissed the shore, the clear untainted air filled my lungs, and the scent of pine and lingering coconut oil lotion wafted around my nostrils. To see the blue sky, filled with splashes of orangish-yellow clouds as the sun made its grand finale took my breath away. It was so peaceful, and the sky looked much bigger there for some reason. Mystifying. No wonder Mom loved it so much.

Cam and I spent every summer of our child-hood there. It was the one place our mother felt safe. And it was where she ran to when she got overwhelmed with city life. My mom had an intimate relationship with nature, and at the lake I saw life in her eyes. True happiness. When we had to close the cabin for the winter, she fell into a deep funk.

Mom didn't get drunk as often there, either – at least not when we were kids. Perhaps Grandma and Grandpa's visits kept her a bit more on the straight and narrow. But once their visits dwindled, then ceased, they pretty much left the cabin to our mother to care for.

I'll give her credit. She took good care of the place because it meant so much to her. But one relationship stoked the fires of her insecurities, and she lost control. She dated the older married man whose cabin was next to ours. After that, our cabin wasn't her safe place anymore. It had been invaded by what she left behind in the city each spring and summer. Because of him – Ken – we were never able to bring her back completely.

I had suspicions at first – nothing solid. I was a light sleeper so I heard Mom leave the cabin some nights when she thought Cam and I were sleeping. I also heard him sneak over to our place: rustles of the bushes outside the cabin... the front door creaking open and closed late at night. But they pretended for the longest time. Pretended their comings and goings were nothing more than friendly neighborly visits – especially when my grandparents were there. They knew too, I'm pretty sure of it. Grandpa got really quiet and Grandma stared at Ken with her hazel eyes narrowed, "tsk-ing" a lot. But as with every-thing else, nobody said a thing out loud. Then one day I caught them.

Cam and I were playing badminton, and Cam lobbed the birdie into the bushes behind our cabin. I looked down between the cabins and saw Mom and Ken whispering. They didn't know I watched from the hill above them. He touched my mom's arm, looked behind him, then kissed her. Now if that was a "neighborly" kiss, I was never going over to their place again.

Anger burned my stomach.

All I could think was, *Ew! He's twice as old as Mom – fat, bald.* And I never saw the man crack a smile. Not ever. Fun for me and Cam.

Mom went on a vacation with him (a real one) shortly after that and Cam and I stayed with our grandparents. To say that our grandparents weren't happy about Mom's new relationship was an understatement. The mere mention of Mom's name during those weeks caused silences so icy we probably could have skated in Grandma's kitchen. Boy, Mom really did it that time. Maybe in her mind she felt that man was a step up. But even I knew he wasn't going to leave his wife.

When they came back from their holiday, Mom and Ken picked us up at my grandparent's house in his car. I refused to go. I didn't even like him just living next door to us at the lake. I saw how he looked at Mom. But I had the satisfaction of knowing he was afraid of my grandfather. Or, at least, it seemed that way. He could never look Grandpa in the eye when saying those polite "Hellos" on the dock.

Ken seemed uncomfortable with me, too. Maybe he just didn't know what to do with a girl. He had three boys, after all. What was he supposed to do with a girl? It really didn't hurt my feelings, because any forced time with him was as painful for me as I'm sure it was for him. But Mom really pushed him on us.

"C'mon, Tam" she'd said. "He could be the one to take care of us. Just try to be nice to him."

Not "He's the man of my dreams," or "I want to spend the rest of my life with this man," or even "I love him."

He could take care of us.

To me, Ken was the worst kind of human being: a wolf in sheep's clothing. I never trusted him. At first, he gave the impression his presence would be what would get our mother to finally help herself. In fact, he even got her to join Alcoholics Anonymous and seek counseling. But he only did that to win my grandfather over. Grandpa backed off, but he never gave his stamp of approval. And neither did I.

What made Ken evil in my eyes was that he took advantage of our mother's fragile state of mind and used it to his own advantage. He caught on quickly that if he encouraged her to drink, she did almost anything he wanted her to do, including things with his friends. I remember the exact night he made his true intentions crystal clear.

It was summertime, so we were at the lake. That particular night, I was stirred awake by music. It was off in the distance, muffled by the thick trees that surrounded our cabin. When I found every light in our cabin on, but no sign of Mom, I threw my clothes on and stepped out onto the porch. It was difficult to pinpoint exactly where the music came from because sound carried and bounced around in our bay. But I had a gut feeling where I needed to look.

Ken had his fishing buddies up for a "man's weekend." In pitch dark, I walked down our long unrailed cement stairs (termed "the stairs of doom" because everyone fell up or down them at least once per summer) and scrambled up the staircase that led to the top of our boathouse. From there, I saw Ken's patio lanterns on. His fishing boat bobbed, tiny ripples brushing against it where it lay tied up between the docks.

Cigarette smoke swirled around the lanterns. I couldn't see what was going on, but I heard enough to give me an idea. Deep laughter. Clanking of beer bottles. Catcalls and whistles. Mom's flirty drunken laugh.

My stomach tightened and I hugged myself. I stomped down the boathouse stairs and continued stomping up to the end of our dock – I didn't even care if they saw me. As I stood there with the cool, glassy water sloshing around our dock, I glared.

There were six of Ken's friends standing around Mom. Glenn Miller played on a small portable stereo while she was passed as a dance partner from one friend to the other. It wasn't fast-dancing to "Boogie Woogie Bugle Boy," either; the dancing was close and invasive. She was so drunk, those men had to hold her up. She wore a small tank top and cut-off jean shorts. She never even tried fighting them off. How could she?

And there was Ken, standing next to a hip-high pile of beer boxes with a smug look on his ugly face. His sweat-stained baseball cap tilted down over his forehead, one hand shoved deep into his pant pocket and the other holding a cigarette between his thumb and forefinger. He brought the cigarette to his lips and sucked hard. The cherry end illuminated his face a suitable red hue for a brief second, then the toxic smoke snaked up past the lanterns.

I knew all those men. I'd seen every one of them at Ken's cabin with their wives at different times when Ken's own wife was allowed to be there. Then Ken saw me. His stance changed from enjoying his show to challenging me to stop it. I took the challenge.

I ran along the path between our dock and Ken's, tiny bushes and rocks scraping my lower legs and the bottoms of my feet, then marched into the center of the middle-aged orgy. I yanked my mother, almost stumbling backwards as she slumped into me, and said, "The party is over."

Every face stared down at me. Not because a pint-sized girl ruined their fun, but more, I guessed, out of fear that I'd reveal their transgressions to their wives. Ken never moved from his spot. The sheep's mask fell off and revealed the Hound of Hell underneath. He took another drag of his cigarette then flicked the butt into the water.

"No worries, boys," he said, with more confidence than he should have. "She won't say a thing. Will ya, Sweetheart? Now go on home to bed. You're a bit young to be here."

Poor Mom looked awful. Makeup smudged, beer poured all over the front of her tank top, and her bare feet showing the signs of bruising as those awful men stepped all over them.

I let her lean on me. "I'm leaving. And I'm taking my mom with me. Oh! And Grandpa will be here tomorrow. Enjoy the rest of your party."

He lit another cigarette, flicking the ashes in my direction. Enough said. The gloves were off between us from that point on.

That night, I finally realized how vulnerable Mom was. As she and I wove through the bushes and struggled back up the stairs to our cabin, falling only a couple of times, my heart broke for her. That doesn't excuse my mother from responsibility. But there was so much proof of the sort of man Ken was, and she wouldn't see it.

"He's using you, Mom." I said the next day.

"Using me for what?" Mom said. "He's got a wife and he's not happy with her. He's just waiting for the right time to leave her so he can be with us permanently."

That's funny. I saw no signs he was leaving his wife. As a matter of fact, his wife bawled Mom out on the dock the afternoon I'd seen him sneak over to our cabin for a kiss – when their relationship was still a secret.

"I know what's goin' on, you home wrecker!" Ken's wife shouted.

Mom laughed nervously. "Excuse me?"

"You two think I'm simple or something, but I know. I've known for months. What kind of woman are you, getting married men to sneak off into the bushes with you? I can't believe you're a child of Wilf and Lillian."

"Uh...clearly you're delusional, lady. I have no idea what you're talking about," Mom said, releasing another nervous chuckle.

Ken's wife's jaw was clenched so tightly the tendons in her neck stood out. "You just stay away from him, you hear? And if I catch him going off again, I'll be talking to your parents."

At first, Mom pretended she didn't care, but her hand shook as she brought her cigarette back up to her quivering lips. What I didn't understand was how that relationship could have been okay with my grandparents. How did they justify all of that?

"Janet will do what she wants to do whether it's good for her or not." Grandpa told me once. "Our resistance only seems to drive her further from us and closer to her wants. Her needs have never mattered to her as much. All we can do is be here for her when it's over. And protect you kids."

Things only got worse after Ken's dance party. He treated Mom even worse, and I wasn't going to let him take over without a fight. Things came to a head one afternoon after a long bonding trip Mom had planned. He'd rented a cabin for the four of us to "get to know one another." Ken belittled Mom the entire time. It was heart-wrenching. Nobody, no matter what terrible things they'd done, deserved to be treated like that – especially not in front of her children.

So the weekend seemed like it went on for a year. On Sunday evening, when we pulled into our parking space in front of our townhouse, Mom and Cam got out of the car. Ken told them to go ahead – he needed to talk to me. A surge of bile sloshed up into my throat.

Mom paused.

She and I locked eyes.

I threw a smile on, to let her know I was okay. She held her hand up and walked home.

Click. The car doors locked. I was in the back seat.

He undid his seatbelt and leaned back in his seat. I looked up into the rearview mirror. His black eyes glared at me from under his base-ball cap. He lit a cigarette, inhaled deeply, then blew a small puff of gray smoke out of the side of his mouth. The rest snaked out of his nose. I hated how he smoked. My eyes narrowed as I squeezed my loyal teddy bear, Ted Brown.

When he finally spoke, his voice was as cool as Ted Bundy's during his trial. "So, did you have a good time, Tami?"

Oh brother. Seriously? "Fantastic time. You?"

"No, I didn't, actually." He took another drag off his cigarette.

"That's too bad, Ken. Maybe you should go on a vacation."

He didn't appreciate my sense of humor. He threw his cigarette out of the window. "Listen you little bitch. I'm the boss now. What I say goes. And soon enough, you're going off to school, and you won't be coming back. Not if I have anything to say about it."

He laughed and lit up another cigarette.

Flick. Puff. Nose smoke.

"You're just like your Mom. You'd better take care of that body of yours when you get older because you won't be good for anything else. Just like her."

That was it. I leaned over the front seat, my eyes focused on his in the mirror, my mouth inches from his hairy ear.

"Let's get something straight. I'm nothing like my mom. I'm not weak, I'm not afraid to stand up for myself, and I will not allow a guy like you to make me feel bad. Mom will never send me away. She needs me too much. She's using you just like you're using her. And, for the record, if you ever treat my mom as bad as you did this weekend, I'll hurt you. I'll tell your wife about you, I'll tell my grandfather about you, and I'll make sure you won't be able to walk around this city or go out on your stupid dock without every-one knowing what a perverted, disgusting jerk you really are."

I slumped down into the back seat, clutching Ted to my chest, my hands shaking and ice cold. My heart pounded in my ears. Angry tears tried escaping, but I refused to allow it. I may have been only twelve, but I knew enough not to show fear. His black eyes didn't move.

Click. I was permitted to leave.

I slammed the door with all my strength and ran to our house. Mom waited by the door. Before she spoke I hugged her for the first time in years. As Ken peeled out of the parking lot like Mario Andretti, she stroked my shoulder-length hair and hugged me back.

Hard.

We missed church weeks in a row. "Those kids need church," Grandma said. "They were baptized and they need to learn about the church so they can be confirmed. Set an example, Janet."

We tried going once, but Ken told Mom we didn't need church. He didn't go. (I guessed it probably burned his skin to set foot through the doors! But I kept that thought to myself.) So Mom stopped going, too. I wanted to go to church, not just because I got to spend time with my grandparents and Uncle Craig. I also missed the inner peace I felt there.

Ken tried to make up for the torturous weekend – not with me, of course. He thought I'd told my mother about our conversation so he tried showing her that he was sorry. There were days of apologies, presents and promises of things to get better and she believed him. I didn't.

Fortunately she only gave him one last chance before things finally ended. Unfortunately, it took quite a scare to get her to that point.

My grandparents went on a trip and Mom, Cam and I stayed in their house. I doubt they gave us permission, but it never stopped our mother before. (I often thought if they didn't want her in their house when they weren't there, they should have taken their house keys back!)

Ken called her several times but he never showed up. A few nights before my grandparents came home, she drank – a lot. I had a feeling Ken was supposed to come over. I got Cam and me to bed and waited. I must have dozed off because I suddenly heard yelling. He was down there. I slid our bedroom door open and listened.

"Please, Ken. Don't. Please stop," Mom screamed.

I stepped out of our room. From the top of the stairs I saw Ken's elbow rise and fall. I ran down the stairs, then froze on the landing. Our mother was on her knees and Ken had a clump of her hair tangled in his hand. He saw me, but continued punching her in the face.

She cried harder when she saw me. "Go upstairs, now!"

"Let her go! Let her go or I'm calling 9-1-1!" I yelled.

I got ready to run to the upstairs phone, but Ken threw Mom to the floor. Then he leered up at me and said, "Look at her. This is your future, you little bitch. You're crazy just like her."

"Aren't you a man, beating on a woman? Get out of my grandparents' house or I'm calling the cops!"

He kicked Mom in the back and stormed out the back door. I watched out the side window to make sure he really left. He did. Forever. Mom went into the kitchen while I was at the window.

"Mom?"

She had her back to me.

"Mom? What are you doing?"

She didn't answer me. Her body shook as she cried. I crept up beside her. She held Grandpa's butcher knife over her arm. She'd tried that many times before – threatening to do it – but for some reason it felt different this time. I was scared.

"Mom, Ken isn't worth this," I said. "Please. Please, don't do this."

She looked down at me with the same look in her eyes she had the day Muriel had beaten her up. Defeated. Lost.

I tried again. "Mom, please. Just put the knife down, okay?"

She dropped the knife in the sink, slumped down to the floor and cried. "What's wrong with me?" she said. "How can I make this stop? I can't stand this anymore."

I put my hand on her shoulder and sat with her until she cried herself to sleep. We never talked about what happened that night again. She told my grandparents some story about "waking up and realizing what a jerk Ken was and that he'd never leave his wife" and things went back to the way they were before.

But that awful man changed something in my mother. She lost the happy, good part of her soul. He took it with him that night.

I still hate him.

Chapter Six

The Gift of Music

Music is well said to be the speech
of angels: in fact, nothing among
the utterances allowed to man is felt
to be so divine. It brings us near to
the infinite.
~ Thomas Carlyle (1793-1881)

I used to call my mother's struggles, "The
Triforce That Is Janet." The Triforce comprised
the three things that made her who she was,
each pulling her mind in a different direction –
fighting for control – her bipolar condition, her
drinking, and her music.

The main, and most important, part of the
Triforce was her creative genius. The extent of
her creativity was limitless. When I was ten, I
found stacks of her poetry in a white faux-
leather trunk in which she kept her old papers
(and *Alcoholics Anonymous,* the Big Book). I

didn't understand what I read at the time, but her work was, I thought, incredible.

Her words were dark, but they swirled deliciously on the page. She didn't write her poetry in straight lines. Some were in the shape of leaves, others went diagonally across the page, and some even gave the illusion of a snake swishing across the white background. She not only had a gift of words, they were artistically arranged so the reader was visually captured from beginning to end.

Other stacks held her sketches, mostly penciled or with dark charcoals. The subjects were often sad, with eyes distant or empty, but they were outstanding considering she'd never had any formal training in art, drawing or sketching. There was a drawing of me with head tilted down, looking up from under my bangs – waist-length hair hugging my body, ankles crossed and hands folded. The look was stern – sullen. Someone else's hand was under my chin beckoning me to look. It gave me chills.

But Janet's greatest gift, to herself or to anyone who heard it, was her gift of music. It has to be said that, despite herself, our mother was one of the best musicians I've ever heard. In fact, there were two things people must know about her above anything else: music was the single most important thing in her life, and she loved her students dearly, and they loved her. It was one of the main reasons I taught myself to play piano, and she helped me move forward with it. I joined the school and church choirs – so she would love me or accept me or – something.

Normally Mom and I fought constantly and had nothing in common, but put music in the picture and it was as though nothing else mattered. The only way to truly know Janet Batty was to be able to relate to her on a musical level.

In everyday events, my mom was insecure and self-conscious. I believe she knew full well something was wrong with her, but she didn't think she had any control over it. And she refused to get help. Imagine how hard it must be to wake up each day and not know if you'll be able to get through to the end without freaking out. But when our mother sang or played the piano, there were no insecurities. The darkness in her eyes disappeared for a little while, and she shone. For just one moment you forgot about what made you angry with her: the booze, the drugs, the outrageous behavior. There, with her fingers dancing across ivory keys, or with a microphone nestled into her tiny hands, she was flawless. She rocked!

Grandma said she knew Mom would one day be a musician after listening to the way she cooed as baby. As Grandma told the story, my mother lay in her crib happily babbling to her stuffed animals, but the difference between her and other babies was she varied her coos and they were on key (Grandma swore to it). So began the legend.

I imagine it must have been difficult for my mom as a child. To be as good as she was, a young musician had to sacrifice many things to practice time. Many of the things of childhood would have been more fun than practice. A serious pianist practiced technique at least one hour, played pieces for one hour, and advanced to four or five hours a day. That didn't include an hour needed for required theory lessons. All of that on top of regular school homework? It must have been stressful for Mom.

Unfortunately, I don't know much about what it was like for her to maintain her gift and still be a teenager. Auntie Lois, my godmother and Mom's closest friend, met her in high school, so, I guess she knows her better than most people do. Auntie Lois became an outstanding contributor to the musical community in Canada. She sang all over the world with the Manitoba Opera, winning awards for her gift. She basically lived the life my mother only dreamed of. My mom could've had the same life. She gave it up for me.

Everyone told me it wasn't my fault, saying she chose not to follow the same path Auntie Lois did. After all, she had no problem leaving us with my grandparents when she couldn't handle life. They would have been "tickled pink" to take us so she could go on tour. Imagine how they would have raved about that!

What our mother didn't realize was that my grandparents raved about her even though she wasn't an opera star like Auntie Lois; even though she never sang on *Hymn Sing* like Auntie Lois' sisters, or performed on *Rainbow Stage* like some of her own students did. She was "just a teacher," as my mom described herself. But she was a great one. And her students adored her.

Grandpa sat in Grandma's green-and-white-checkered barrel chair and listened whenever my mother played on their baby grand piano. I watched him. He rubbed his hands on the arms of the chair and rocked as the music flowed from the piano keys to his soul. Grandpa was hard of hearing in his later years, but never once did you see him cup his ears with his hands to hear her play. He felt it. And every time she played, Grandpa wiped his eyes when she finished.

Every time.

Another gift was the gift of voice. Our mother and Auntie Lois used to sing duets in the school and church choirs. I never heard them perform together, but from what others have told me they were magical. As time went on, the booze and the tar from the cigarettes took a toll on Mom's singing voice, and she was only able to teach piano, but I'll always remember her singing – when she sang to me at night when she didn't think I was awake, when she sang in church – until she couldn't sing anymore.

If you've ever seen *The Sound of Music* and heard Mother Superior sing "Climb Every Mountain," that was my mom. She played the piece on the piano and sang along, and when she would strike the last chord of the piece, there was always a long silence before the applause – not because she sucked, but because her talent literally stunned people. I saw that happen often.

Her children have each inherited one or more of her creative talents. We have our individual strengths, but we each play instruments, write, draw and sing.

I have a picture of me sitting on her piano bench when I was all of two. I sported wild curly blonde hair and sunglasses too big for my face. A trained musical eye could see my small hands were in perfect position on the keys. I was so lucky.

Our mother was troubled, and she hurt me more times than not, but her gifts to me are something for which I will always be grateful. We sang in choirs together (I was soprano, she was alto). We played duets for her students as an incentive for them to practice.

I argued with her when she forced me to practice when I'd rather go out. I guess she saw something in me that I didn't. It was the only level we seemed to relate on – and that in itself was a miracle – because the way to my mother's heart was through music.

My only wish would have been that on days where all three forces were fighting for supremacy in her mind, she had the strength to follow the music.

Maybe it could have saved her.

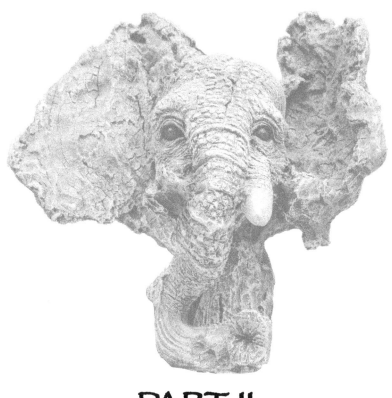

PART II:

GIVE LOVE
ANOTHER CHANCE

Chapter Seven

Daddy #2

Physical infidelity is the signal, the
notice given, that all fidelities are
undermined.
~ Katherine Anne Porter (1890-1980)

After Ken, Mom did her best to pull her life
back on track. She signed on more students,
took up yoga and jogging and even tried giving
up smoking. She chewed a lot of Dubble Bubble
bubble gum during that time as a way to work
through cravings.

"I'm doing great," she told my grandparents,
and anyone else who asked. Personally, I think
she tried too hard to convince them. I wasn't
buying it. I couldn't stop thinking about the
night Ken left.

The image of Mom with the butcher knife
wavering over her wrist stole my thoughts while
I was awake and invaded my dreams when I tried

sleeping. I got up every few hours just to make sure she was still in the house, and when she wasn't there, I checked the knives in the kitchen drawer before I was able to go back to bed.

I considered hiding them.

I decided that seemed a bit obsessive.

That's when I made a deal with God. I wasn't sure if he'd go for it but I tried: *If she wants to die, please, just take her. She'd be happier up there with you, anyway. We only seem to make things worse for her down here. If you want her here, please tell me how to help her, and us. Otherwise, just take her. Because watching her slowly kill herself is torture.*

Amen.

I hated the early Eighties. I was a pre-teen with a boy's body, Cam became obsessed with hockey (I hated hockey), and my mom was moving into her thirties. All of a sudden the hippie lifestyle wasn't as acceptable anymore – no more free love, excessive partying and multiple sex partners (at least, that's how it was in Winnipeg, Manitoba). Women demanded independence and equal treatment in the business world. Well, all women that is except my mom.

Mom was on a mission to find a husband. Not because she wanted one but more because Cam and I were older and more expensive to take care of. She needed help. I wanted to believe she was tired of being alone and needed companionship. Not so.

I told my mother to find someone for herself, not for us. Cam and I didn't need another official

Daddy. We had our devoted grandfather and Uncle Craig, and I knew in my heart that my birth dad loved us from somewhere, too. We were blessed the way things were.

"Just find a guy that loves you," I remember telling her. "Don't search for a dad for us."

She didn't listen. She drank more and worried more. Our medicine cabinet, over-crowded with cold medicines, aspirins, and other over-the-counter drugs, helped her suffocate the pain she felt. She stopped taking care of herself the way she used to. And, because we were older, she left us alone more often instead of calling a babysitter to take care of us.

Though her search for a suitable dad for us was noble, it lacked research. Her choices were questionable even before she'd met Ken. A great example was Edward – a name that makes me shiver even today.

Edward's face is a blur to me now, but I remember him as tall, pin thin and old – I mean really old. He was older than Ken, at least twice my mother's age. What bothered me the most about him was that the guy was never sober. Edward's claim to fame was he once drank a Texas Mickey in just a few days. Yes, I saw what my mom desired in him. Yuck. Mom and her friends were party animals, but when I saw a Texas Mickey – a three-liter bottle of rye whis-key – my stomach hurt.

I never liked him from the first lingering hand-shake. "Well, hi there, Pretty Little Lady," he purred after Mom introduced us. "Your mom's told me a lot about you. But she didn't tell me how beautiful you were."

He squeezed my hand then traced my palm with his middle finger. I pulled my hand out from his and shoved it in my armpit. I looked over at Mom. She said nothing, but fidgeted for a few seconds then ushered me out of the room.

I hated being near Edward or even talking to him. His breath always reeked of cheap whiskey and cigarettes. One evening, Mom took Cam to a hockey practice. Edward showed up just before she left and offered – perhaps a little too enthusiastically – to stay with me until she got home.

She looked at him. Then turned to me. What I wanted her to say was, "No, Edward. You're six sheets to the wind. I am too embarrassed to take you in public with me and too scared to leave you with my child. Go home."

What she said was, "Yeah, okay. That'll be fine. There's stuff in the fridge to eat. I'll be home in a couple of hours." She hugged me and left.

Edward and I were alone.

He leaned in close to me when the inside door slammed shut. "So, Sweet Pea. What do you wanna do?"

"Nothing," I ran up to my room. It felt like I'd been up there for hours, and would have stayed up there until someone got home, but I got hungry. The television was on. I hoped he'd passed out.

He sprawled on our couch, his fingers tucked into the front of his pants behind his Texas-sized silver belt buckle. His other hand wrapped around a bottle of Jack Daniels, three-fourths empty. He must have brought that with him, because Mom was a rum and wine drinker.

It amazed me he didn't have a drinking belly the way the other party guys did. I stood at the bottom of the stairs staring at the top of his balding head. I had to walk by him to get to the kitchen. He didn't even move when I walked to the kitchen, but on my way back to the stairs with a snack in my hand he sat up.

He gestured beside him. "Come sit here and have your sandwich. I don't think your Mom wants you to eat upstairs, does she?"

I looked down. "No."

"Here," he said, putting his bottle on the coffee table. He patted the cushion beside him. "I don't bite."

I stood there with my peanut butter and honey sandwich. My heart pounded in my ears. I hadn't felt that way since Chris lured me into my closet. Whether I sat with him on the couch or went up to my room, the events that followed would have happened anyway. It was worse than what happened with Chris because Edward knew what sex was and, by the tender age of twelve, so did I. My naïveté was gone a long time before that night – Mom had sex with many guys with her door open or right out on the couch so we saw more than we really wanted or needed to. Mom and Cam came home soon after Edward had finished. He polished off his whiskey then passed out as the theme song from *Fantasy Island* came on. My peanut butter sandwich was squashed into the carpet.

I bled for two days and tried keeping it from Mom. I was too scared to tell her. Edward told me he'd do the same thing to Cam or kill my mom if I told anyone. But I woke up one night with stabbing abdominal pain, and it hurt to pee. Then my mom found a pair of my underwear in the laundry that I'd tried shoving in between piles of clothes. Just like with Chris, she didn't ask me what had happened but took me to the doctor. There followed two weeks of invasive tests a young girl should not have to endure, well beyond peeing in a jar. I had my first internal examination and later was admitted into the hospital for some test where they had to stick a camera into my urinary tract. The diagnosis was PID – Pelvic Inflammatory Disease.

"Mrs. Laird, we need to ask you a few questions," the doctor said in the recovery room.

She went over to the side with the doctor and, even though I couldn't hear everything, my mom's voice got louder as the doctor pressured her for a reason a twelve-year old girl had a condition "you can't get without sexual contact."

"I have no idea," she said, shoving my clothes on me. "Maybe she's just a tramp. Looks are deceiving, you know. I'll deal with this."

Nice. At that point, I didn't give a crap if Edward made true to his promise to kill her. Better him than me. But I still had to keep quiet for Cam. So I did.

Even though there was no discussion about what really happened, Mom dumped Edward the day after I got home from the hospital. He didn't take the break-up very well.

He became obsessed with Mom. He hung out in front of our complex and watched our townhouse. My mom was good friends with Edward's sister, Miriam, who lived a few doors down from us, so he still had an excuse to be around.

He started following Cam and me to school – we saw him outside the fence during recess, and he stood on the corner when we got out at lunch and after school. It got to the point where Cam and I were so scared we literally ran to and from school every day.

One night while drinking with Miriam, Mom unintentionally made a wise decision. She threatened to hire a private detective to follow us to make sure Edward didn't hurt us. After that, Edward left us alone. I still felt his presence, though, because I had to be on medication for my PID. This time it was a cream I had to insert with a tampon-like instrument. It stung worse than the event that caused the infection, and for two weeks I couldn't get the ugly scene out of my head.

I didn't blame Mom. The guy had tons of money, but Mom wouldn't sleep with him, so he took the next best thing, in his eyes. He was sick. Good came from it though: she never left us alone with anyone like that again. And even though she was still promiscuous, she never brought her dates/boyfriends to the house again – until she met my stepfather, Pat.

No one is exactly sure how my mom and Pat met, although Mom went to high school with Pat's older brother, Don. She and Pat dated for a few months before Mom brought him home to meet Cam and me.

When he was finally allowed to come over, I knew right away he was different from the other guys. He actually sat with Cam and me and asked us questions. Not just the stupid, your-mom-is-forcing-me-to-talk-to-you questions like, "So, how old are you?" He asked us what we liked and shared stories with us.

The first time Pat came over, Cam sat on the floor organizing his ever-growing hockey card collection. I was playing piano. Our piano was on the left of the entryway into our townhouse. I didn't notice him at first as he stood in the doorway listening to me play. When I finally noticed him, I stopped.

"No, don't stop," he said. "That was incredible. You're very talented."

I shoved my hands under my thighs. "Thanks."

"The gift of music is a powerful thing. I play a little guitar and sing."

I smiled. "Mom didn't tell us that."

After a little more chit-chat about him being in a band and our mutual love of certain bands, like The Beatles, Eric Clapton and The Rolling Stones, we moved into the living room where Cam sat stacking his hockey cards for the millionth time.

"Hey! What an awesome collection," Pat said. He and Cam chatted about hockey stats and players for a while. He said he'd bring over his Intellivision set (a very early video game session with *Donkey Kong* and other 1970s and 1980s games) the next time he came over. He really seemed like he was interested in getting to know us – both of us. And never once did I feel threatened by him or scared to be alone with him. He was so nice, I felt guilty. He had no clue what was in store for him.

During the beginning stages of their relationship, Cam and I were seeing our dad every second weekend. These visits weren't consistent because he was always stationed out of the country – exotic places like India, Pakistan or Germany, or he was made to feel his presence wasn't wanted or needed. Whenever our mother found herself in a desperate situation and needing money, she contacted Dad to "give him another chance" with Cam and me. It was like having my heart ripped out over and over again, just like that time when I was five.

Cam never seemed affected by our visits with Dad – he took it all in stride. But I found it so hard to say goodbye. It never mattered whether our visits went smoothly or not. Whenever he dropped us back home, I ran up to my mom's bedroom window and cried while I watched his beige Rabbit hatchback drive away. For those two days, we were away from the chaos in our house, and with someone who just wanted to have fun. He paid attention to us. I don't know if she was jealous or what, but one weekend, my mom had enough of my crying at the window.

"You act like you'd rather live with him than me," she said. "Besides, how do you think it makes Pat feel to have you bawling for your dad when Pat is here actually doing stuff for you? Huh? C'mon, Tam! Think of someone else besides yourself."

"I *would* rather live with him," I screamed. "I *hate* it here!"

Before I had a chance to run up to my room, she grabbed me by my upper arms, put her face right in mine and said, through gritted teeth, "Well, then. Why don't we ask him if he'll take you, huh? He's still in the driveway."

She dragged me by one arm to the front steps and waved him back. She told him to sit on the couch. "Okay, then. Tell your dad what you want."

I couldn't believe she did that. Not only did she put me in the position of choosing between them but she did it in front of Pat, who had been sitting there watching TV the entire time.

"C'mon, Janet," Pat said, leaning over the chair. "Don't do this."

"No! She has a problem being here with us and has something to say to her dad and she's going to do it," she said, lighting up a cigarette. "Okay, we're all listening to you," she said, blowing out a thick cloud of smoke. "Talk!"

My eyes burned. My chin quivered as I tried to repress the angry tears rising. I looked from one person to the other. "I...I...want to live with you, Dad."

My dad shot my mom a side-glance and rolled his eyes, "I really wish you could, Tam. But I'm going on another out-of-country station. I wish things were different..."

"Forget it," I said. "Forget I even said anything, okay?"

I ran out of the room. I heard Mom say something about me being melodramatic, Dad asking what was really going on, and then, a few minutes later, the front door slammed. I cried for hours.

A couple of weeks later, when my dad brought us home after the next visit, Mom went out to his car after we got into the house. A few minutes later, Dad's car sped out of our semi-circle driveway, his tires screeching as he turned onto the main road. That marked the end of our visits with him.

Just before she and Pat got married, Mom told me our dad didn't want to see us, and didn't want to give her money to take care of us, so she forbade him any access to us. Because we didn't know any better, we believed her. After a while, I resented him – I thought he gave up too easily. I blamed him for leaving Cam and me with someone who clearly couldn't even care for herself, never mind two children. But Pat softened a lot of my anger.

A couple of nights after the last time we saw Dad, I heard Pat and my mom down in the living room. Neil Diamond was on the stereo, so I knew what was up. I woke up while they were just talking, but they were both drunk.

"Ever think about getting married?" Mom asked.

Oh no, I thought. *Say "No!" Pat!*

A brief silence followed her question. I thought it was going to go unanswered. Then he said, "Sometimes, I guess. Why? Do you want to get married?"

Holy crap! I wondered if he saw the entrapment unfolding.

"Are you asking me to marry you?" Mom asked.

Another brief silence.

I always thought Pat knew early on what my mom's plans were. He made a huge amount of money being a programmer at a respected university, and had awesome benefits. That's all she wanted – someone who could take care of us.

So, Pat responded the way he was supposed to. "I wasn't, but I can."

She whispered. "Ask."

It was like an excruciating scene from a really bad soap opera with no remote to change the channel. Ugh!

"Janet, will you marry me?" Pat asked.

She answered with an overenthusiastic, "Oh Pat! Yes! Yes, I will!"

I heard lots of kissing, then Mom suggested he come up to tell me. I never slept through the night, and being awakened at 3:00 a.m. wasn't unusual. I played along, though. I pretended to be asleep.

Pat sneaked into my room. I felt his weight tilt my mattress to one side. He gently shook my shoulder. "Tam? You awake?"

"No."

"I have something important to tell you."

"What?"

"Your Mom and me are getting married."

I tried not to laugh. "Welcome to the family, 'Dad.'"

I pretended to go back to sleep. My thoughts raced as Neil Diamond got louder downstairs. She'd gotten what she wanted. It didn't matter that she didn't love Pat. She landed a man with a great job, excellent benefits and awesome pay. And, to boot, he got along with us.

Perfect.

Part of me felt so badly for Pat. The other part of me thought, for such an intelligent guy, he had to be the dumbest person in the universe for not seeing what she was doing. He did it for Cam and me. He even asked for my permission to adopt us after they got married. I said it was okay. I mean, we weren't really "Lairds" anymore at the time. He saw how devastated I was about the absence of a relationship with my dad, and he knew how close I was to Grandpa. He just wanted to play a fatherly role in our lives, too.

I still thought he was stupid for getting involved with my mom. But I had a lot of respect for him for being there for Cam and me.

It took several months for my grandparents to warm up to the idea of my mom marrying Pat. I'm not sure why but Grandma, in particular, gave off a frosty aura. Pat, God bless him, tried to thaw the Arctic air in the house whenever we went over for a visit, but it never seemed to work. Pat did have a bad habit of over-talking. You know, like never giving a person a word in edgewise? And he didn't have very much of what my grandmother called "couth."

Pat looked like an average-height Grizzly Adams. His dark hair and beard were always on the longer side and unkempt. His teeth, and some of his fingers, were stained yellow from years of smoking. His wardrobe was stuck in the

1970s – polyester shirts with wide collars, and his personal hygiene habits, to put it as politely as possible, weren't always the best. Okay, he wasn't exactly Tom Selleck, but he was good to me and Cam. I thought my grandmother was often unfair about him.

Grandpa tried keeping the waters calm. He made small talk with Pat while Grandma just ignored him. I didn't understand Grandma's response. Pat had to be a step up from Ken and the rest of the loser parade my mom marched through their house! Finally, though, peace talks were held, and Mom gave my grandmother full wedding-planning rights.

The arrangements went forward, but in my mind, Mom just didn't seem excited the way a normal bride-to-be should have been. She was calm, and showed no real emotion – not excitement or happiness or jitters. Nothing. Her lack of enthusiasm seemed to go unnoticed by everyone around us. It made me nervous because I had a gut feeling that something was about to explode. It was just a matter of time.

Pat and his family loved to party as much as Mom did. They drank hard and in excess – so our mother fit right in. I guess being with someone who partied the same as she did seemed to make everything she did okay. So, when Pat's family offered to throw the rehearsal dinner the night before the wedding, a knot tightened in the pit of my stomach.

From the moment we got to the house of Penny, my aunt-to-be, Mom pounded back one drink after another until she was completely inebriated. I begged Penny to let us stay the night there, but she refused.

"There's no way I'm going to allow this to become a habit. Sorry Tam," she said, shaking her head. "Just call me if you need to talk."

Fine, I thought. But someone had to drive us home and there wasn't one person there who was in any shape to do it. Our future Uncle Don, the person who always partied the hardest, volunteered.

The plan was that Uncle Don would drive Cam and me home safely and go back to get our mom, who was still at Penny's place arguing with Pat's mom. Pat, who was more sober than Don, had to play referee between the two women.

"You don't love my son," our future Grandma said. "You're using him for security."

Mom laughed, sucking hard on her cigarette. "You're just pissed off because he won't be 'Mama's Boy' anymore."

The whole scene felt so wrong. I didn't want to be driven home by someone who probably saw two of me. But I sure as hell didn't want to stay there, either.

"How are you going to force her to come back here?" I asked. "She's not going to get into a car with you."

Don belted out his famous belly laugh that sounded a bit like The Joker from the old *Batman* TV show. "Well, if she doesn't come gracefully," he said, gulping down the last of his rye and water, "I'll pick her up and carry her into the fricking car. Don't you worry. I won't let anything happen to you. Or her."

Just as I was about to refuse his offer, our grandmother-to-be slapped my mom so hard it silenced the room. As Mom tumbled backwards in a rather *Dynasty*-fashioned catfight way, I rolled my eyes, turned to Don and mumbled, "Let's go."

So, I let this man, whom I'd known for all of a few hours, drive Cam and me back home. Surprisingly, the ride was calm. He must have had a lot of experience driving home pissed drunk. He pulled up in front of our townhouse.

"You guys'll be okay, right?" he asked, a cigarette hanging from the side of his mouth.

I slammed the car door and grabbed Cam's hand. "We're fine."

He didn't respond. He stayed there until Cam and I were safely inside and he saw me wave. Then he went back to get Mom. I secretly hoped and prayed he wouldn't come back.

It was already 2:00 a.m. when Don dropped us off. I poured Cam into his bed, then slipped into my pajamas. I tried staying awake but failed. At about four I startled awake to loud thumping from the living room. Thinking Cam and I were still alone I got up to investigate. As I crept down the stairs, familiar grunts revealed the source of the noises. I just thought my mom and Pat must have been doing some early celebrating. I was wrong.

I gasped and it seemed my thoughts screamed out. *Oh, no! It's not Pat! It's the wrong man!* I could hardly make my feet carry me back to my bed, and my mind kept saying, over and over,

My mother cheated. My mother cheated right before her wedding.

Oh how I wanted to rat them out, they totally deserved it. But I didn't. I kept their secret. My stomach churned.

I didn't sleep that night. The next day while Auntie Lois, Mom, and I primped for the wedding – Auntie Lois and I were bridesmaids – Mom put on her happy face like nothing was wrong. I didn't speak to her. I couldn't even look at her.

Uncle Rick took pictures of the wedding. I posed in the car, in the family photos, and in the wedding party pictures. I refused to smile.

"C'mon, Tam," Uncle Rick kept saying to me. "At least pretend you're happy." *Ugh – if he only knew.* Nausea gripped my stomach like a vice. I wanted to tell someone what was going on, but I didn't know who to turn to. Pat looked so happy. I didn't want to ruin it for him.

The music started. The guests filed into the banquet room to witness the union. Auntie Lois and I walked down the aisle. My body shook. When Auntie Lois sang during the ceremony, her rich alto voice filling the room, I fought back tears. I couldn't let this go on. It was a farce.

I knew my mom didn't love Pat enough if she could cheat on him the night before their wedding. It was doomed from the start. I tuned out most of the vows. I just didn't want to hear them. They meant nothing. Then the minister said, "If anyone here has just cause why Janet and Patrick should not be married, speak now or forever hold your peace."

I scanned the room. People fidgeted. Grandpa instinctively took Grandma's hand. I looked at Don. Pat looked at Mom, adoringly. Mom's mouth quivered in the silence.

I know a good reason! I know!

I needed to speak up. I opened my mouth to speak but the minister spoke first. "By the power vested in me..."

I lost my chance. My silence forced me to live with feelings of guilt stabbing me in the stomach. Every time I looked at Pat, I knew. Every time our mother acted like the devoted little wife, I knew. Whenever Don came over and he and our mother locked eyes, I knew. I hated them for putting me in that position. I hated myself for not speaking up. And I hated God for making me witness it.

A waitress handed me a fruity kid drink after the ceremony while the bride and groom did their rounds. I didn't want some stupid kid's drink so I made Uncle Don get me a flute of champagne instead. I didn't expect him to actually bring me one, but he did. I didn't know what was stranger – that I was only thirteen and drinking champagne, or that Don didn't seem to see any problem with it.

Whatever. He owed me. I took a deep breath then gulped down the bubbly liquid. The bubbles went up my nose, making me cough, but I drank it anyway. I don't know how many I had but my eyes blurred at about four glasses.

Over the next several years, I would be in that state many times.

Chapter Eight

Babies, Mohawks and Mayhem: The Honeymoon Is Over

I have been on the verge of being an angel all of my life but it's never happened yet.

~ Mark Twain (1835–1910)

My mom and Pat spent their honeymoon at the lake – rather bold I thought since Ken still had his cabin next door. Cam and I stayed with our grandparents. At the end of the week, Cam and I had to join our "parents." I didn't want to go. The night before we had to leave, my grandmother came to tuck me in. I got to stay in Mom's old bedroom.

"Grandma, please don't make us go," I begged her, squeezing her with all my might.

She squeezed me back and patted me. Cupping my chin in her palm, she said, "Now, stop this kind of talk. Why wouldn't you want to go?"

I couldn't give her a solid reason why Cam and I were better off with her – at least not one that I felt like talking about. Going to the lake didn't bother me. I just didn't want to be stranded there if something bad happened, like Mom taking off and Pat having to go find her.

Oh well, I reasoned. *How bad could it be?*

I don't even remember now who ended up driving us out there. The only thing I remember was trying not to puke the whole time. Cam and I held hands for the entire two-hour drive. As the car climbed the small hill leading to the cabin, I figured things couldn't get worse.

I was wrong.

The parking area was filled with cars. There were beer bottles, cans and caps, cigarette butts and empty booze bottles all over the normally beautifully sculpted yard. I counted six of our new cousins running around wild and destroying the summer stuff Cam and I looked forward to playing with each year. And, added to the scene, Uncle Don was on the roof of our cabin sitting in a lawn chair watching a football game because "the reception was better" up there.

He wore an oversized straw hat, mirrored shades, a t-shirt he must have gotten when he was in high school, and a bathing suit that was way too small. He leaned over when he saw me, his beer belly bulging out from under his shirt, and raised his beer to me. It was like a scene from *The Trailer Park Boys*.

That was my brand new family.

I didn't know whether to laugh, cry, die of embarrassment or ask for a beer – which I was positive someone would have gladly passed me. I smiled weakly at Uncle Don. He stood up. Good thing for him the roof wasn't very slanted. He raised his beer over his head and hollered in his best Billy Graham accent, "Ah ba-leive. Hallelujah an' praise tha Lawd. Ah've been blessed with tha powa of tha almighty beer. Say it with me now. Hallelujah! I don't hear you, young sista... Hallelujah!"

Wonderful. What a way to show Cam and me – eleven and thirteen, respectively – how to feel pride about the colorful fibers that wove all that was Nicol – our new heritage. I left Cam bent over in hysterical laughter while I went into the cabin. I was relieved that Grandma didn't see our cabin in that state: backpacks, people's clothes, water toys, and garbage all over the place. And some teenaged guy with red hair lay passed out on our couch.

Suddenly, Don's voiced bellowed down the chimney. "Ho-Ho-Ho. This is your summer Santa. I'm mighty thirsty from all my gift-giving. Is there an elf down there who can bring me another refreshing beverage?"

"I'm guessing you aren't referring to a glass of juice," I screamed back up the chimney.

Uncle Don responded with his Joker-styled laugh. "Only if there's a few shots of rye in it to kill off the healthiness."

I rolled my eyes and poured him a "three-finger drink" just like I was taught.

On my way to deliver Uncle Don's drink to the roof, I tripped over someone's backpack and spilled some of his precious drink on my shirt.

A gut feeling told me this might be a regular scene.

Years down the road, Pat told me he wanted to leave my mom the first few months into their marriage. Like many before him, he couldn't handle the fighting, the erratic behavior, and the inability to stop her from hurting herself, or me and Cam.

I understood.

It rips your heart apart when you can only sit and watch the person you love self-destruct. It was like Chinese water torture. Each time my mom went manic and tried fleeing, another drop fell on our foreheads. The drops got faster and faster and faster until we wanted to scream, "Enough, already!"

But Pat stuck it out. Partly because he wanted to, and partly because he had to. He was loyal to us and wanted to be there. And my mom got pregnant.

I was fourteen. I don't remember the pregnancy very well, but our mother wasn't one of those "glowing and happy to be with child" types of women. She didn't like being a baby pod. From what I knew, even the most even-tempered woman is negatively impacted by the foreign baby hormones flowing through her veins. Imagine how it must have been for someone already in a highly emotional state. I'll give it to my mom, though; she kept it together most of the time. I was proud of her. There were a couple of incidents where she lost control and drank. And it gave me insight into what it must have been like for my father many years earlier. We tried keeping things calm for her. We tried keeping her, and us, away from alcohol, but it wasn't always possible.

One time at the lake, when I stayed behind in the city to work, Cam told me that she'd driven to the liquor store in town begging for a bottle of rum. She was already drunk, and I guessed Cam tried getting rid of the booze for the sake of our sibling-to-be.

Despite all the odds, Heather Ashley was born, healthy and happy, on October 9, 1984. Heather's birth marked a lot of new things in our lives. We moved two doors down from my grandparents, to a nice house rented from family friends. New baby laughter filled our home. I loved that house, even if it wasn't really ours.

With an infant to care for, I hoped my mother would settle down. Not so. It started just two weeks after Heather was born.

Mom and Pat went to an office party, and I babysat for them. She promised they wouldn't be late because of how exhausted she was. When the wee hours of the morning crept in, I knew our new chapter wasn't meant to be: Mom came home drunk. And, from what it looked like, she tried finishing a fight she must have started.

"You are such a loser," she said, her speech slurred. "Don't you think he's a loser, Tam?"

I refused to answer. She went on a half-hour-long tirade about how unhappy she was, and how she needed a break but never got one. She threatened to leave, had to be forced back into the house, then took a few swings at Pat before he'd had enough. He shoved her in self-defense. She spilled onto the floor in her usual over-dramatic fashion.

I finally moved off the landing to intervene because I didn't want Heather to wake up. Cam, who'd been hiding in the kitchen, sprung out to break up the fight. Mom was already back on her feet, coming at Pat again. Cam jumped on her back to restrain her, but she was freakishly strong for such a tiny woman. It took Cam and Pat to get her down on the floor where they held her until she stopped screaming.

This became a familiar scene – at least once a week. My memories of the times from after Heather's birth to the birth of my younger brother, Ian, are scattered. My own mental health started breaking down. A person can only go on for so long with no sleep, constant chaos at every turn, and growing insecurities normal to puberty.

I knew people saw the bruises, the bite marks, the occasional black eye or fat lip. But nobody ever asked – just like when I was younger and went to school with blood all over my clothes.

I would have asked. I would have wanted to know if that girl needed help.

That's when I started cutting myself. I hid my new habit under long sleeves. I wanted to feel something besides anger. It never got serious. I had nicks from shaving my legs that were worse. Once a week – usually after my mom had an episode – I just took a razor blade and skimmed it over my arm a few times. Just deep enough to see a line of blood rise to the surface. When the pain went away, I put bandages over the wounds and pulled my sleeves down. It only lasted for a few months until Cam caught me – the one time I forgot to put bandages over my cuts.

He grabbed my arm. "What the hell is this?" he asked, holding up my sleeve. "You tried to kill yourself?"

I tugged my sleeve down. "No. Don't be stupid. I'd do something a lot more effective."

Cam's eyes rimmed with tears. "Shut up. If I see anything like that on your arms again I'm telling..."

"Who? Mom?" I laughed, wiping my nose. "Go right ahead. Then I'll tell her you smoke weed in the basement. Oh! That's right! She already knows about that! Just like she knows about my arms. Nobody cares, Cam. Nobody."

He punched me in the arm. "I do."

We stared at each other, then hugged. We were afraid of losing each other, but never talked about it. We were both time bombs waiting to go off.

How did we get like that? That beautifully naïve boy I protected from everything. Suddenly, he did drugs and partied just as much as our mom did. Kids my age bought drugs from Cam and his friends. That was how he dealt with what happened around us. Cam felt that he couldn't fight it – he told me all the time – so he joined it. I couldn't protect him anymore. In fact, he stepped between my mom's fist and my face a lot back then. The scary thing was, he wouldn't stop hitting her until someone took him off her. His anger was disturbing.

I just drank.

And cut.

It numbed me. Kids at school made fun of me because I cried inconsolably when I drank. Many people told me to quit drinking or learn how to handle it. Understandable. Who wanted their good time ruined by a blubbering fool?

In addition to my creating this reputation for myself, someone circulated a rumor that Heather was my child and my mom was raising her to protect me. How that got started, I have no idea. I wasn't exactly a person who could hide a pregnancy. I don't think I hit 100 pounds until I was in my twenties.

One morning I decided it had become too much for me. I didn't want to feel anymore. I was tired of being a protector, a liar, a loser, a parent. So, I had a shower, brushed my teeth then swallowed an entire bottle of aspirin and went to school. It took about an hour before my body reacted.

The bell rang for morning classes to switch. As I walked down the narrow hallway voices echoed in my ears. Everything swirled around so fast – suffocating me. A shrill high-pitched scream filled the hallway. People stopped and stared. They pointed. At first, I didn't understand why everyone was at a standstill – until I realized the screams came from me.

The pills in my system caused me to hallucinate. A girl I'd never talked to before helped me up, took me to the nurses' office and stayed with me until someone came to take me to the hospital.

"Good luck trying to get hold of someone," I said. "Nobody's sober. Nobody gives a shit."

The nurse said nothing. "Just don't let your-self fall asleep, Dear. I'll be right back."

I enjoyed the light pins-and-needles sensation spreading all over my body. A tremor nestled into my right leg. It felt odd watching my leg jumping spasmodically and I wasn't moving it.

So tired. Just a small nap.

"I'll bet this must be really enjoyable for you," I said to my rescuer. "Funny, huh? Loser Tami gets loaded again."

She stared me down. "You don't know what I'm thinking. I don't have a problem with you."

I forced a laugh. "Whatever. I've heard you talk about me. Look, just get lost. I'm not interested in making guilt friends right now."

"Your problem is you are so determined to be alone you don't realize there are people around you who actually do care about you. You just don't give anyone a chance. I understand. Just know that, okay?"

With that, she left. I turned my head back up to face the ceiling. The tremor in my right leg jumped to the left. Pat burst into the room. He tilted his head at me then put his hands on my legs. I didn't bother asking where my mom was. Obviously she didn't want to deal with it.

Pat told me she didn't believe I did anything. I was just "trying to get attention" and she wasn't going to buy into it. It was probably better she didn't come. It would have been another excuse for her to drink.

I begged Pat just to take me home, but he didn't listen. He took me to the emergency room at St. Boniface Hospital. Pat briefed a triage nurse about what I did, how many pills I took and how long they'd been in my system. Then another nurse, who I guessed dealt with suicidal teens too much, guided me to a huge room with three beds sectioned off by curtains.

After pulling a curtain around one of the beds she barked, "Lie down here."

My legs still shook but I lay down as ordered. The nurse took my pulse, stole some blood, then handed me a tiny vial of brown, syrupy liquid. "Drink this," she said, writing something on my chart. "It's going to empty your stomach so we know how to treat you."

"This is going to make me puke? No way! I'm not taking it," I said, shoving it back on her tray.

She bent down with the vial right under my nose. The pungent smell reminded me of Jack Daniels. "You either drink this stuff or I'm going to shove a tube down your throat. What's it going to be?"

I took the vial. The nurse stood there until I swallowed the foul vomit-inducer. Then she put a small plastic bowl beside me and put her hand on my shoulder.

"It shouldn't take long to work, judging by your size and the amount of drugs you took. Use this when you start to vomit. It's for your own good."

I lay there and waited. A commotion stirred behind the curtain next to me. A husky voice begged for help. Another voice – a mother? – told the victim's story:

"She's been down for quite a while. We had her on antidepressants. We thought they were working, but I came home from work to see her...she was in the tub with blood all around her. We thought it was just a phase...that things would work themselves out...you know how teenagers are. If we'd known things were this bad..."

It's funny how people always say that in retrospect: "If I'd only known." I wondered if my grandparents thought my mom's problems would "work themselves out." And I wondered whether my mom felt that way about me.

Then the room fell silent.

The voices faded as they stepped out of earshot to discuss the girl's treatment. I wanted to go and peek behind the curtain. I wanted to talk to that girl, to ask what her story was. She whimpered, "Oh God, why? Why don't you just let me die? I can't do this anymore...it hurts to be here...hurts..."

Part of me understood where that girl's feelings stemmed from; the other part of me had a lot of experience to maybe help her in some way. I wanted to reach out to her, but the brown potion swirled around in my stomach.

The girl's bed creaked and I heard her shuffle across the floor. Surprised they didn't restrain a person who wanted to die that much, I looked around for a call button – something to call for help. I couldn't move. My stomach lurched.

God, someone come back! Help!

Just as I tried getting out of bed to help the girl, my stomach released. Everything I'd eaten for the last day splattered all over the sterile gray tiled floor. Then something glass smashed next to me. I knew what was happening. I knew what she tried to do and I couldn't help her. I fell to my hands and knees unable to stop the vomit from spewing out. I tried crawling to the curtain. I didn't make it. I collapsed.

Behind the curtain, my young neighbor squeaked a weak cry of pain, gurgled then fell on the floor. It reminded me of a bowling ball landing on a soaking wet towel. Her bloody hand fell under the curtain. I didn't want to look but I had to.

I saw her. Just before the nurse picked me up from the floor, the girl and I locked eyes. A scene forever burned into my memory: she'd slashed her throat. I couldn't see the gash but I saw blood saturating her blonde hair. She must have been beautiful. When she saw me, she let out a sigh, then smiled.

She was free.

Amid the screams of loss, and failed attempts to regain control of my stomach, I mourned the girl. I saw her beautiful tortured face many times later on in my life. She never knew how in taking her own life she saved mine.

My near-suicide was never discussed again. My mom didn't talk to me for two days after I got home. I don't think it was because she was angry but more because she didn't know what to say to me. It wasn't entirely her fault. I knew that. But things were getting worse.

Scarier.

A couple of weeks later I came home from a babysitting job to find Mom sitting on the couch staring out the living room window while Pat took a stern stance behind her: arms crossed, feet apart, no facial expression.

"What's up?" I asked.

Unusual. Both of them were sober on a Saturday night. Apparently, Cam had missed his ten o'clock curfew – by three hours. My stomach jumped into my throat. Before I could ask why they weren't out there looking for him, red lights flashed around the living room like a hellish strobe light. My mom still didn't move from her position on the couch. I pushed her head out of my view to see Cam being helped to the door. He was loaded – and only thirteen. Pat opened the front door. At that time, our house was across the boulevard from a youth detention center. How convenient.

Cam had thrown up all over himself; puke was running down his face. His clothes were muddied and he'd ripped holes in his jeans. His fists were both badly smashed up. Officer Campbell gave my mom and Pat two choices: "You can either take responsibility for him or we can hold him overnight in the Youth Center across the street. What's it going to be?"

Officer Campbell had obviously lost patience with Cam. I think Cam puked in the guy's cruiser.

Cam looked up at the policeman and slurred: "Fuck you, ossifer Cam," then broke out in hysterical laughter.

Officer Campbell wasn't amused. Neither was Pat. Mom never moved from the couch. Pat finally spoke. "We'll take him. Thank you, Officer."

Pat poured Cam into his bed, puke-stained clothes and all, (which Pat made him clean the next day). He told me to go to bed too. He left my mom in the living room. I turned off the lights. She didn't flinch.

I stared at her for a few seconds before going up to my room. I hated that damn beast inside of her. I wanted to shove my hand into her head and pull it out. She was losing her battle with it. Like the girl in the hospital, my mom was giving up.

After Cam, Pat, and I retired to our rooms that night I made a decision: I was still going to fight and I would win. I got the scissors from the bathroom and chopped a huge chunk of my hair. All the things that floated in my head for the last few months flooded my brain and flowed down my face with every hack.

Don and my mom.

Chop!

The nameless girl in the hospital.

Chop!

Cam's drug problem no one acknowledged even when he was brought home by the cops.

Chop! Chop!

That – thing – constantly torturing my mother. And the booze she used to quiet it.

Chop! Chop! Chop! Chop!

Breathing hard, with clumps of my hair all over my shoulders, feet and dresser, I looked at my new hair. The sides were cut to my scalp, the middle stuck up three inches and the front hung down to my chin.

Perfect.

I took eyeliner and drew Cleopatra-style lines around my eyes. Grandma would hate it. I'd just calm it down when I was around her.

The new me.

Watch out.

Chapter Nine

It All Went Down On Niagara Street

The gods visit the sins of the fathers
upon the children.
        ~ Euripides (480-406 B.C.E.)

My suicide attempt was never talked about
again; not even between Cam and me. Like
everything else, it was added to the mountain
under the rug. The White Elephant grew another
inch. But it proved that the problems in our
house weren't just my mom's anymore.

Cam now expressed things overtly with anger
and violence: he punched holes in walls, he beat
up friends when they tried cutting him off at the
end of a party. Once he even head-butted the
stained glass window in our front door. His tem-
per was scary. It was worse when he was high or
drunk. He stopped letting me protect him after I
got out of the hospital – when he realized I
wasn't always as strong as I pretended to be.

And poor Pat. He had two messed up teen-agers without any real structure or supervision, two babies to worry about, and a wife who wasn't able to care for herself most days, never mind her children. He had to work late and work on weekends to make up for all the times he left early or took off from work, either to find Mom or to help us clean up her messes. He became harder on us, but I developed a tremendous respect for him.

He tried straightening us up. He set up rules and made us follow them. He stayed in contact with our schools to make sure we weren't skip-ping out, and if we got caught we were grounded. He never yelled at us or hit us, he just spoke his mind in a calm, controlled way. I could see he hated what was going on, but he repressed his anger, and I feared that one day he might snap. I tried my best to make sure I stayed under the breaking point.

One night, he had to come and get me after a party. I was fifteen. It was a weekend tradition for all of the local kids to crowd into Richardson Park for a huge party. Drugs and booze were passed around, and it didn't matter how old you were. I don't know how much or what I had, but I was out of it. The normally cool party went out of control when fights broke out around the park. I heard someone yelling, "Holy shit! The cops are coming!"

Lights flashed, sirens blared through the park, and everyone scrambled. I was so out of it I couldn't scramble. People running by shoved, bumped, and pushed me out of the way. Then, a flying beer bottle smashed open a girl's head and she fell on me, knocking us both to the ground. Blood gushed from her wound and onto my shirt. I screamed. No one heard me. Everyone was running and screaming around us to get away from the cops.

Cam grabbed the girl off of me. Her blood was smeared all over my chest and face. Cam recognized her as his best friend's girlfriend. He yelled, "Get the hell up and get out of here! I have to find Robin."

He stumbled into the darkness with the girl. I ran with the crowd. As I bolted out of the gate, a cop grabbed me and said, "Young lady, are you okay? Are you hurt?" I didn't answer. I just ran and ran until my thighs hurt. I have no idea why he didn't come after me.

I didn't recognize where I was. The cool air and the adrenaline rush weren't enough to clear my head. It was well after midnight and nothing was open. I stopped off at the first house I saw with the lights on and rang the doorbell. An older couple opened the door and I burst into tears.

I must have been a fright: A scrawny girl with a fire-engine-red Mohawk standing a foot above my head, with Cleopatra eye makeup running down my face. My clothes were covered in mud and blood (and most likely beer stains), and I was shivering from the cool fall night.

"Please," I said, my teeth chattering. "I'm lost. Can I please use your phone to call my dad?"

Ten minutes later (apparently I was only a few blocks from my house), Pat came to get me, apologized to the couple and thanked them, and took me home. We didn't speak the entire way to the house. No lectures. No speeches about being too young to drink. Nothing.

I ran into the house, sped past my mom who was passed out on the couch in front of the TV, and straight up to my room. I shut my door and hugged myself. What was happening to me? Why was I doing these things to myself? Did I have what my mom had?

I caught my reflection in the dresser mirror. A crusty patch of dried blood the size of a butternut squash stained my favorite Duran Duran shirt. I burst into tears and ripped it off of me, throwing it in the garbage. I rubbed dried blood off my arms and face with eye make-up remover pads. I put on my pajamas and there was a knock at my door.

"Tam, it's Pat," he whispered. "Can I come in?"

I opened the door, expecting a smack or a lecture. He hugged me. I was confused. I thought, *You just came to pick up your underage, obviously drunk teenaged step-daughter, with blood all over her, from an old couple's house she didn't even know and all you're going to do is hug me?"*

"Cam just got home covered in blood too. He went downstairs – said he didn't want to talk to me. I'm not going to ask what happened. I just wanted you to know I'm glad you're both home safe." He pulled away, saying, "You're better than this, Tam. You're better than *she* is. You can control it. Do better. You have younger siblings watching you. Let them see they can do better too, by setting an example."

For some reason, I started thinking about my dad again. Certain periods of my life I thought about how different my life would have been had I been raised by him rather than Mom. Then I thought of how Mom forced me to talk to him that day when I was younger, and how he had said he couldn't take me. I didn't want to feel that pain again.

Not too long after I got out of the hospital, I began speculating. Where was he living? Did he think about me? Was he out there wondering how Cam and I were doing? Did he regret giving us up so easily? My close friend Colleen suggested I look him up.

"Just see if he's here," she said. "If he is, you can call him or go see him or something."

The thought excited but terrified me at the same time. I so wanted to make the connection but was scared he didn't care anymore. So one day at school, when we should have been in math class, Colleen and I looked up Dad's name in the phone book. And he was listed! An icy explosion burst in my stomach. How could he have been in the city all that time and never once tried contacting us? Then I remembered how he and Mom left things. She wasn't exactly open to the idea of having him around. I think her last words to him were, "No money, no access."

I didn't have the courage to call him, though. I hadn't seen or spoken to him in over eight years. So much had happened and changed. I changed. I decided that writing to him was a better choice. I could speak my heart but still have the option not to send it. Once things are spoken, it's not as easy to erase...or throw away.

I don't remember exactly what I said in my letter, but I know I told him about Heather and Ian and flowered things up with how life was going for Cam and me. I didn't think he needed to know all the details right away. I gave him Colleen's address to reply to.

"I'm sorry," I wrote. "If Mom knows I'm contacting you, it could get ugly. And I most likely won't get your letters."

After keeping the letter in my canvas bag for over a week, I walked over to the mailbox across the street from our house. I stood there for what felt like hours with the letter in my shaking hand. Then I took a deep breath, pulled down the creaky door and dropped it in.

I was in a state of high anxiety for the next several weeks. Just when I thought I'd made a mistake, wishing life had a rewind button, Colleen called me when she got home from school. "You got a letter!"

A few hours later, I was sitting on her bed staring at the messy handwriting on the front of the envelope. My heart pounded. I chewed the inside of my cheek and picked at the skin around my thumbnail. Colleen came into her room with a lit cigarette and two huge glasses of amber liquid, one of which she handed to me. I was so grateful in that moment that her mom was working.

I winced at the drink but eagerly grabbed the cigarette. It wasn't habitual for me but something I did when I was nervous...or drunk. "It's

Southern Comfort and iced tea," she said, "...and really strong. Now gulp it down and open that damn letter!" I took a long drag of the cigarette, blowing out half of the gray smoke and making O's with the rest. Then I took a huge swig of Colleen's beverage, gagging on the strength of it, put my smoke in the ashtray and ripped open the envelope.

It has been a long time so I don't remember his exact words, and the letter is long gone now, but it was awesome. His writing was big, messy and beautiful. He told me that he was happy I wrote to him, and surprised. He explained that he did try contacting us when he came back into the country, but Mom wouldn't let him see us. He decided it was best to keep his distance and that, somehow, he knew we'd find him when we were ready. He met and married an amazing woman and they lived in a small house on the opposite side of the city from us. The most amazing part of the letter was how he closed it:

"You are very brave contacting me, Tami. How hard that must have been for you! But I'm glad you did. Yes, I would love to get together when you're ready. Let me know and I'll meet you. Thank you for contacting me.

Love, Dad"

I cried. Colleen hugged me. We got drunk on way too strong Southern Comfort and iced tea drinks, smoked a lot of cigarettes, then I went home, put my letter in my school books and passed out.

I was happier than I'd been in a long time.

After that, Dad and I spoke a couple of times on the phone, from Colleen's, of course. Then we decided to meet in person for lunch. I met him at a downtown restaurant. It was nice. Initially, I think he was shocked by my Mohawk and dark Goth look, but he said I reminded him of my Auntie Jeannie, his sister, who was always unique. We talked about so many things, but not the past. Neither of us wanted to go back that way yet. So I just enjoyed my time with him.

I got to experience being happy for a little while. Reconnecting with that missing piece of my life brought some balance. I was actually going to classes, doing homework.

Then it happened. I made a fatal error: in my rush to make my bus one morning, Dad's first letter fell out of my school books. And Mom found it. I came home from school that day and my Aunt Debbie (Don's wife) met me at the door. I knew instantly something was wrong. I felt a film of sweat under my arms and my heart pounded in my throat.

"Tami, I think you should go somewhere else for a while," Debbie said in a loud whisper. "Your mom..."

"Is that her?" Mom said, her tongue barely able to make the words.

Heather and Ian came around the corner, each of them hugging one of my legs. I didn't say anything. Aunt Debbie stared at me, her eyes wider than I thought possible, nodding towards the door. I probably should have gone. I had an inkling what would happen next. But I just couldn't leave Heather and Ian with my mom when she was like that.

Mom suspected something was going on. I was spending a lot more time over at Colleen's. I was happy. That wasn't allowed without her knowing why.

She came around the corner, holding onto the wall. "Well, look at you. Welcome home. You like living here?"

I didn't answer her. I felt my brother and sister's arms squeezing even tighter around my legs.

She tried letting go of the wall, but she stumbled into Debbie, who held her up. "I don't think you do. Otherwise you wouldn't have contacted Bill. Did he finally say he'd take you?"

I still stayed quiet. My mind raced trying to think of how to calm the situation. I wondered what had triggered things this time. It couldn't have been *just* my stupid letter. I saw a pile of bills on the kitchen table.

She shoved Dad's letter in my face, it was crumpled in her fist. "What the fuck is *this*?"

I tried grabbing it, but she pulled it away, stumbling backwards. Heather started whining. "It's none of your business," I said. "And it's mine."

She started laughing. "What? What was that? Did you hear that, Debbie? It's none of my business!"

Debbie swallowed and hugged herself. Mom ripped my letter into tiny pieces then threw them at me. Confetti fluttered down onto Ian and Heather's heads. Heather burst into tears.

"Listen here, you bitch," Mom said. She sauntered towards me, using the wall for support.
"Everything you do is my business if you live in
this house. And this man doesn't give a shit
about you. Not one tiny little shit. How did it
make you feel that he was living here all this
time and never *ever* contacted you?"

I glared at her. Of *course* she knew he was
there all that time. "He told me..."

"Shut up!" she yelled. Ian started crying. I
peeled the kids' arms off my legs and gently
pushed the kids towards Debbie. Mom backed
me up against the screen door. She put one of
her hands beside my head and the other she
pushed into my chest. "He's a fucking *liar*! And
you're just like him." Her hand squeaked as it
slid down the glass of the door. She kept pushing
it back up.

Debbie said, "Tami, uhm, your mom told me
that you have a physio appointment right now
for your ankle. Why don't you, me, Heather and
Ian go so your mom can rest?"

I'd hurt my ankle in gym class and needed
physiotherapy, but had to postpone the last
several appointments because Mom had been
in one of her up moods, finding other things she
needed to do instead. She'd been drunk the last
two appointment dates.

"No," Mom said, her face right in mine. Her
breath smelled like a bathroom that hadn't
been cleaned in months. "I'll take her. Get me
my keys."

I pushed my mom back. "There is no way I'm
getting in a car with you. Get away from me."

She pushed herself right into me. "You're just like him. You going to hit me now?"

That was it. I knew she was pushing my buttons, that's what she did, but I couldn't stand there and say nothing. "Fuck you!" I yelled. Debbie took the little ones back into the living room. I heard them screaming in unison. "Maybe I am like him. But I deserve to know or find out! *You're* the liar! And he didn't come here because of *you! Leave me alone!"*

I shoved her away from me as hard as I could. She stumbled backwards, knocking the wind out of her for a moment as her back hit the wall. Her face went red and she gritted her teeth. I braced myself. She came at me and punched me in the face. My head bounced off the screen door and she punched me again in the mouth. I crumpled to the floor, pulling my body into a tight ball with my back facing her. She kicked me in the ribs once, picked me up by the back of my collar and the bottom of my sweatshirt and tossed me down the front stairs. My head hit the cement and I saw stars.

"You want to get to know him? Then go," she screamed. "Get the hell out!" I lay on my side on the sidewalk and cried. I dragged myself to Colleen's house. They were eating dinner at the time so Colleen told me to wait in her room in the basement. While I waited, I heard the phone ring. A few minutes later, Colleen came down, fighting tears.

"Your mom just called and told my mom that you came here because you got into a fight with someone and you took off. My mom wants you to go home, Tam. I'm so sorry. Your mom basically made it sound like you were a drunk and had problems. So my mom doesn't want you here, or for us to hang out."

I saw my face in Colleen's mirror. I had a fat lip, a black eye and a goose egg bump on the side of my head. And *she* made *me* look like the bad guy. I stood up to leave and Colleen hugged me. I winced. My side hurt where mom kicked me.

"I know what happened," she whispered. "I'm still here for you. No matter what my mom says."

I cried uncontrollably for several minutes, letting Colleen hug me. Then her mom called from upstairs saying that I had to go. I wiped my face, straightened my clothes and walked back home.

When I got home, Mom was passed out on the couch. Pat was watching TV. Heather and Ian were safely tucked into their beds. I had no idea where Cam was. My room had been completely trashed – my jewelry box dumped out, all of the toiletries Mom or Pat bought for me, gone. All my Duran Duran posters ripped off my walls. All the clothes in my dresser and closet thrown around.

I had to stop contact with Dad – for everyone's sake. I gave him a brief explanation. I didn't have to go into too much detail. He seemed to understand.

"Call me when you can, Tam," he said. "I'll be here."

I didn't talk to my dad or hear from him again for another eight years.

But I was allowed back in my mom's house. For now.

Mom started seeing a psychiatrist. She told me she chose to see one because she needed to talk about her adoption, her marriage and her PMS (that's what she believed was the root of her problems at that time). But instead of giving her a complete assessment, the psychiatrist just prescribed antidepressants and Valium.

What no one realized at the time was that putting a bipolar sufferer on antidepressants can be compared to putting a violent person on steroids: it magnified the underlying problem. Also, since my mom still drank while on her meds, her episodes become longer, more violent and even more unpredictable.

Around that time, my mom began searching for her birth parents – perhaps at her shrink's suggestion. Pat fully supported the search because he figured it would help Mom deal with a part of her past and, in his naïve optimism, thought it would help her to get better. We all hoped it would help. Maybe, we thought, if she had answers to her lifelong questions about why she was given up, it would heal the open wound of abandonment that she still felt.

I understood Mom's need to figure out where she came from. Maybe her discoveries would help me understand why I was the way I was, too. I was messed up and had no clue how to feel anything other than sadness, anger and loneliness. I walked around the high school halls holding back tears every moment. I didn't seem to fit in with any of the crowds, whether the headbangers, the dope heads, the preppies or even the geeks! I was self-conscious with my skinny, underdeveloped body and acne. I barely spoke to anyone unless I was drunk or high, and tried my best to avoid eye contact (which probably stemmed from really bad eyesight, but rebelling against eyeglasses.) I was known at school as the "skinny chick with the funky hair."

I guess it could have been worse. I felt lost. I dropped out of high school at sixteen. Pat made it clear that if I wasn't going to school, I had to get a job. I was the neighborhood babysitter and made good money from that, but I needed a real job too. Grandpa helped me get a job at Bassey's Pharmacy.

"Jim Bassey isn't going to give you a job in his pharmacy when you walk in there looking like a clown," Grandma said. She hated my new look.

But Mr. Bassey didn't mind my Mohawk, eyeliner, black ripped-up jeans, Beatles t-shirts and Doc Martin boots (even in the summer) or my black nail polish and bright red lipstick.

"I've watched ya grow since you were a tot," he said at my interview. "I know you're a good kid. Hair grows back. Makeup washes off. Your soul never changes, and yours is golden."

Mr. Bassey reminded me of my grandfather with his strong but quiet presence, his generosity and subtle sense of humor. He gave me my first job and helped build my self-esteem during a time I needed it. I worked there for a year before I took another job that paid more money.

Quitting Bassey's was difficult, but he was kind and understanding. It was a frosty autumn Sunday evening when we closed up the store together for the last time. We stood next to each other counting out the cash. The only sound was the clanking of change and flipping of the paper bills as they slid through his long, white fingers. I was riddled with guilt. I always had trouble with goodbyes. His parting words to me still ring in my ears to this day:

"You're an honest soul. Never let what surrounds you affect who you become or what you do. Listen to what your heart tells you and let the rest go. I know you'll do great things. I can see it. You need to see it, too."

With that, he wrapped his arm around my shoulder and squeezed, pulling me into a comforting hug. As I walked home, tears stung my eyes. For some reason, I knew I'd never see him again. It hurt. But I never forgot him or his kindness.

He passed away not long after that.

I dreamt about her a lot – that nameless girl in the hospital. For two years after my forced visit in the hospital, I had nightmares every night: the blood, the screaming, the yearning to save her...I woke up in cold sweats night after night. At seventeen, I took the dreams and what Mr. Bassey said to me as signs that I needed to pay more attention to the things that were most important. Important things, and people, that I hadn't been paying enough attention to – like my grandparents, and my faith.

We began to worry about Grandma's health. It was subtle at first – a forgotten name here, a missed appointment there. We all knew something was wrong, but we figured she was on too much medication. One day I opened up the cupboard to grab the salt and I must have counted at least seven different bottles of pills prescribed to her.

Why would one woman need so much medication? I thought.

I knew that she suffered with arthritis and was always in pain. Seeing all of those pills sent a shiver down my spine. She was the only mother I ever knew. I spent a lot of extra time with her. In the summer when I worked at the pharmacy, I stayed with her and Grandpa while everyone else went off to the lake. My grandparents helped me to redirect my life.

I had to attend confirmation classes. Actually, I didn't *have* to, but I promised Grandma I would get confirmed. As she reminded me, "You were baptized in the Protestant church and, as long as there's a breath in me, I'll see you're confirmed there as well. After you're confirmed, you can do what you want."

I did it for her – at least that's what I said. I think I believed a lot more than I let other people know. It hurt too much to admit my dedication to my faith. All summer, I attended my classes, reviewed Bible passages with Grandma and prepared for initiation into my congregation. That fall, the weekend I was to be confirmed, my mom joined our neighbors to have a yard sale. It was so profitable cocktails were mixed – *way* too many cocktails. My parents were tanked. I wasn't surprised, but I was disappointed.

The next morning in church, Mom and Pat sat in the middle pews beside my grandparents. Mom still looked drunk, but she beamed with pride. I sat in the front pew with the rest of my class. I never made friends with any of the other kids. We were all about the same age but I just didn't have any desire to befriend anyone. I was doing it for Grandma. That's it.

I looked up at the marvelous stained glass window. I tried avoiding His stare. There He was just like when I was a child snuggling in Grandpa's armpit – the mid-morning sun lit up His eyes like blue fireflies.

When it was my turn to read a passage from the Bible, I searched the room. There, all in the same row were my parents, my uncle, and my grandparents. I focused on Grandma. She dabbed her eyes. In my seventeen years, I'd never seen her cry. Not one tear. I knew nothing else in my life would mean as much as what I did at that moment.

I wanted to run from the pulpit and forget the entire thing. I felt dishonest. How could I stand there before God and the congregation and say I accepted Christ into my heart after all the doubts I'd had over the years? How could I put on this charade when I cursed God and blamed Him for everything my family was going through? I closed my eyes, stopping the floods rising in them. I felt gentle pressure on the top of my head – as if someone placed their hands over me. The feeling was powerful yet calming. I repressed a shiver.

When I opened my eyes, Grandma held her Kleenex to her heart and Grandpa gave me a "thumbs up." I read my passage then nodded at Grandma – as if to say, *Everything will be okay.* Later that afternoon, Grandma gave me a beautiful gold cross on a long box chain. She did up the clasp behind my neck and straightened the chain on my chest. She held my hand over the cross and said, "No matter what happens from now on, keep this close to your heart. Nothing happens in life you aren't supposed to experience. God and I will always be there if you wear this and remember what it symbolizes."

I threw my arms around her sturdy shoulders.

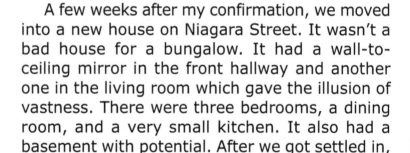

A few weeks after my confirmation, we moved into a new house on Niagara Street. It wasn't a bad house for a bungalow. It had a wall-to-ceiling mirror in the front hallway and another one in the living room which gave the illusion of vastness. There were three bedrooms, a dining room, and a very small kitchen. It also had a basement with potential. After we got settled in, life went on – with the same old problems.

Pat and Mom fought about money again. After I eavesdropped one night, I figured out that when the huge stock market crash happened, Grandpa lost a lot of money. I never found how much, and never asked, but it must have been significant. Mom used to tell me how when she visited him after the crash, he sat there with his head in his hands and wondered how he was going to take care of him and Grandma.

What it meant was that he had to sell something to save their financial stability. Something worth a lot of money: the cottage. There was no way he could afford to pay two mortgages. My mom, of course, wasn't going to let strangers buy and live in her sanctuary – whether Ken was still across the bush or not. So, somehow, she talked Pat into taking over the mortgage for the cabin *on top* of the house mortgage.

How they managed to get the credit, I have no idea. But paying two mortgages definitely put a strain on their already shrinking pocketbook – not to mention their deteriorating relationship.

Since Pat's income was what paid for the house and the cabin, my mom felt trapped. She still taught piano and took in a few more children for daycare but seemed to feel her contribution meant nothing. When she felt trapped or overwhelmed, she ran. She started running more often and for longer periods of time.

On top of all of that, Cam's anger towards Mom escalated to the point where if she even looked at me wrong, he jumped on her. It was even worse when he drank. One night I was terrified into the realization that my dear little brother needed help.

My mom was invited to a choir party. Cam, my oldest childhood friend Susan – who stayed with us for the weekend – and I all went, too. We figured, *How much trouble could Mom get into at a party with church choir people?* As we piled into the car, she was vague as to where we were going. That should have sounded alarm bells for us right off the bat.

We pulled up in front of an old red brick two-story building in an older area of River Heights. The bottom floor had ritzy clothing stores none of us were either rich enough or scrawny enough to shop in.

Before we asked, Mom said, "It's up there. On the second floor." She pointed to three large black-tinted windows on the second floor.

A bar?

Cam scoffed. "What kind of church has a choir party at a bar?"

His faith was destroyed a long time ago. A self-proclaimed atheist by then, Cam said the only reason he went to church was because he was in the choir – yes, we both sang in the church choir despite everything. We loved music. Plus, he loved being in the choir and liked the company of the other choir members.

I shook my head and stared at the sidewalk. Mom had already opened the door. Susan put her hand on my shoulder and squeezed. At least I wasn't alone this time. And, unbeknownst to Cam and me, we finally had a witness. Thank God.

The door opened to a narrow, dimly lit staircase with blood-red carpet. I shivered. Our footsteps clunked on the old stairs and the wood groaned and creaked as each of us climbed to the top. The bar itself was rather intriguing.

To the left of the staircase were the "Guys" and "Gals" bathrooms. To the right was the bar. It reminded me of one of those old Beatnik bars: the walls were painted jet black with the exception of the silver trimming around the tinted windows. The lighting was dim except for the bright lights in the bar in the middle of the wall. Each table had a Sandalwood-scented candle burning and a tiny hand-written menu with the drink specials. Even the ashtrays looked like artwork from the Sixties with their psychedelic colors and amoeba shapes. There was also an open stage with a karaoke machine. An acoustic guitar leaned against a music stand.

We grabbed a table against the wall close to both the stage and the bar. Mom lit a cigarette and said, "Okay, what can I get for everyone?"

Susan's jaw dropped. "You aren't serious, are you? We're all underage!"

Mom took a drag of her cigarette so deep her cheeks sucked in. "You're close enough. Do you want something? It's okay if you're with an adult. Tell you what, I'll get some wine and you guys can drink if you want. Okay?"

Susan was determined to stop things before they got started. "But Cam is only fifteen, Janet."

Mom waved her hand at Susan as smoke wafted out of her nose. "Ah, this place doesn't care."

"Let me guess," Cam said, slumping back into his chair and laughing. "*You* suggested this place, didn't you, Mom?"

Some of the other choir members showed up but not many. Like our family and Mom's friends, people at the church avoided functions where she and alcohol would be together.

Oh, please, God. I prayed. *Please let us get home safely.*

Mom started with wine, moved to rum and Coke and within a couple of hours started ordering doubles. Cam, Susan and I tried our best to make sure she didn't get all the alcohol she ordered. We made a plan – admittedly, not a very good one – to take turns drinking her drinks until she ran out of money. What we forgot was that her tolerance was much higher than all of ours put together. And what we also didn't know was that Mom had an open tab on her credit card. When I started seeing double, I had to stop.

"If I drink anymore," I said, "I'm gonna puke."

Even Cam couldn't drink any more. Susan stopped much earlier than we did, so we had to take her turns. Mom didn't stop. Then she did something I never forgot: she sang. Normally, I didn't mind. But when the bartender got out from behind the bar, grabbed the acoustic guitar and played the opening to "The Rose" – one of our mother's favorite songs – I cringed.

She sucked. She sang off key, forgot the words, her voice was so vibrato her head shook and she wasn't even able to stand straight. My heart broke for her. She didn't see how her illnesses were destroying her beautiful talents. When she finally finished, no one clapped. No one. Even Cam was speechless. We had to get out of there. Cam and I couldn't drive, and weren't in any condition to drive even if we could, but Susan had her Learner's Permit.

"Susan," I said, grabbing her hand. "Do you feel confident enough to drive us all home?"

She rolled her eyes at me. "I can try. Will she give up her keys?"

"Not a chance," I said. "But she doesn't have a choice."

My mom wouldn't leave. In fact, she argued with the bartender about getting more drinks. He felt she'd had enough – she disagreed. He closed her tab, gave her back her card and told her to take us home. That's when she blew up. She cursed at the bartender. She swung at the waitress and threw herself on the floor, refusing to leave, just like a child.

Susan was scared. I got her to focus on me. "Susan," I said, giving her the car keys. "Go open up the car and start it up. Cam and I will find a way to get her out of here, okay?"

Susan disappeared down the staircase. Cam yelled at Mom to get up. She swore back at him. I went up to a mountain of a black bouncer, who'd been watching us – expressionless – from behind his mirrored sunglasses, and I asked him to help me get our mother out of there.

He leaned right into my face. Normally, I would have been frightened, but he put his meaty hand on the side of my face and said, "Something tells me this isn't the first time this has happened to you. You let me deal with the hard stuff this time, okay? And if you ever need a shoulder, you come back. I'm always around."

I believe God sent me angels at different times of my life. That was one time. And although I never took him up on his offer, I never forgot that wonderful bouncer. I hugged his hand between my shoulder and cheek, and squeaked out, "Thank you."

He went over and told Mom to get up, three times. She chanted something inaudible under the jazz music that the bartender blared to tune her out. After the third non-response, my bouncer angel effortlessly picked her up off the floor. She went limp as a ragdoll to make things more difficult. He flung her over his shoulder.

As he thundered down the staircase, we ran to keep up with him. He recognized Susan and stomped over to our car. I opened the door for him and he threw my mom in the back seat. She was still chanting something I couldn't make out.

Cam got in the back with Mom and I sat with Susan in the front. She gripped the steering wheel so hard her knuckles turned white. I put my hand in her lap. "It's okay, Susan. You can do this."

She teared up. "No. I know I can drive. I'm just – oh Tam. I'm just sorry I didn't believe you whenever you told me about your mom. I'm so sorry. I wish I could help you. Help her."

"You are helping," I said. "And you're helping her, too. Just say a prayer for her when you go to church tomorrow, okay?"

She put her hand over mine and squeezed. Mom kicked my seat and muttered. I made out the words, "God forgive me. I am your servant." I couldn't understand the rest, but it sounded a lot like the passage I'd read at my confirmation ceremony.

Cam lost it. *"Shut up!"* he screamed. "Shut up, shut up, shut up!"

Cam punched and kicked Mom with every "shut up." She didn't make a sound. She just kept chanting. I tried my best to stop Cam's punches. Susan broke into tears.

"Just drive, Susan," I yelled over the chaos. "Get us home."

Susan drove at a snail's pace, but we got home safely. I ran in the house to get Pat. I gave him a summary of what happened. He ran out to the car, told Cam and Susan to go in the house, then dragged Mom inside. Pat dropped her on the floor in the front doorway then turned her head just in time for her to puke all over the floor.

God bless Pat. He sat with our mother for a good five to ten minutes as she continued throwing up. Then he took her to bed, cleaned up the mess and gave me a hug.

Susan never slept over again, but she finished her B.A. in Family Counseling.

That night in the bar changed something in Cam. His anger towards our mom grew stronger. Perhaps it was a desire to protect me, because whenever she was manic *and* drunk she lashed out at me. Cam threw himself between us and beat the crap out of her. He had no patience for Mom's tirades, and would completely lose it whenever she'd had an episode. It was around that time, at Christmas, things got so bad Cam rammed the stained glass window in our front door with his forehead. He split his head open. He still has a scar.

Chapter Ten

Losing the Battle

Reward her for all she has done.
Let her deeds publicly declare her
praise.

~ Proverbs 31:31 (NLT)

My eighteenth birthday came. Mom gave me
a bottle of rum. I had only one drink from it. She
had the rest. My birthday fell on a Sunday that
year, so she wanted to start early by taking me
out for birthday drinks.

"Since you can legally drink now," she said.
"I want to take you out for your first legal drink.
How does that sound?"

Scary as hell, I thought. She and Pat had
been fighting about money, and almost everything else, so I knew she was all charged up.
After the choir party incident, I don't know why
I even considered going out with her, but she

made the effort to dress up – something she didn't do much anymore as she'd gained weight. So I reluctantly got into a nice pair of jeans and a sweater, threw a bit of makeup on and joined her upstairs.

On our way out, Pat said, "You guys look like 'Before and After' pictures."

Mom scowled at him and I pulled her out the door before it got any worse.

Long story short, the evening ended pretty much the same way as it had at the choir party. We went to Grapes – the same place we'd gone for my tenth birthday, only they'd built a bar on the side of the restaurant. We had a couple of drinks. She started ordering doubles. I stopped drinking. She started hitting on a really old guy who entertained us with his war stories from World War II. She got out of control and refused to leave. Only that time I was alone with her.

The manager caught me on my way out of the bathroom and asked me if I wanted a ride home. Normally, I would never have taken a ride offer from a guy I didn't know but, for some odd reason, I felt safe with him. There was no real conversation in the car, but he did offer his phone number in case I ever needed to talk. Another angel God sent to watch over me.

Since we took Mom's car, Pat went back to Grapes with the manager. It took three men to get my mom out of the bar and into the car. Then she came home and fought with Pat until she passed out.

Pat started tape-recording her rants as proof that it wasn't all in our heads. I'm not sure whether Mom knew about that, or if Pat ever let her listen to them, but they were just as upsetting the second time around.

It was becoming predictable. It could be days, weeks, sometimes even months between incidents, but they were always scary, dangerous and involved my mom drinking for days. It was like a cycle for which we never could identify a beginning. I even went to the library to research her "symptoms" (since there was no Google at that time). I was always directed to something called "bipolar." It would be years – in University – before I researched it fully and understood.

My birthday party was actually very nice – tame compared to past birthdays. Uncle Craig and Dorothy were there, Grandma and Grandpa, Pat, Heather, Ian, Cam, and my friend Colleen. Susan couldn't make it. I didn't even have a boyfriend to share the celebration with.

I'd never been interested in dating. I made out with guys at parties, but never allowed myself to get more serious. First, I had no desire for the intimacy or sexual stuff in relationships. The only time it didn't terrify me to be touched was after I'd had a few drinks. I figured that only led me down a path of being considered "easy" if someone just liquored me up. The other reason was I just didn't think there was a guy out there strong enough to deal with all the crap in our house – take me, take my family! And I didn't want to dump my situation on another person. So I kept guys, and everyone else for that matter, at arms length – allowing them only so close, letting them know me only a little.

I had a lot of guy friends I hung out with, but nothing ever got serious. In fact, I officially "lost" my virginity with a close friend of mine, Jamie. He was going off to University in Toronto, and I knew I'd never see him again. So, one night I told him, "I want to lose my virginity with you. I want you to just take it with you, so I never have to think about it again."

He knew a lot about my past – the rape, the sexual abuse, my mom. He knew I wasn't being flippant or disrespectful about it. I just wasn't into the whole "Save it until I meet Mr. Right" stuff. At that point, I simply didn't believe there was a Mr. Right. Technically, my innocence was gone a long time ago – taken from me by some disgusting, perverted old man who most likely drank himself to death – but shame and fear took its place. I just wanted my real "first time" to be with someone I trusted, who "got" me, and who'd make the whole event what it was to me: a passing.

So, we did it, he left and that was it. The entire thing was actually a relief to me because I'd felt like I'd been faking something for so long. Jamie helped me let that tiny part of my past go, and I will always hold a special place in my heart for him. The last time I saw him was a couple of days before my eighteenth birthday. He gave me a card, kissed me, then said, "See ya, Tami. Stay on the lighter path. No matter what has happened to you, you are so much more."

I opened the card after he got in his car and drove away: *Time together will always be treasured. Love, Jamie. XO*

Mark was the first guy I actually dated. I met him a few weeks after Jamie left. He was what I called a "safe" guy because he was unofficially seeing another girl who was away at school. We hung out, went to the bar, lay on the beaches, drank, and had sex. I don't think I really felt any heart-swelling love for him. And my mom hated him. Not only because he took me away from the house when I didn't want to be there, but also because he stood up to her. That, and he was mulatto. Dating him brought out a disturbing side in my mom that I never knew about her. Or maybe I knew but didn't notice.

One night when I came home from watching movies at Mark's house, she was up waiting for me. She was so drunk she swayed while she was sitting!

"Have fun?" she asked, struggling to find her cigarette in the ashtray right in front of her.

"This is old, Mom," I said, tossing my shoes in the shoe rack. "I'm going to bed."

"You let that guy touch you, don't you," she said, finally finding her smoke and sucking a huge drag from it. "Those ugly black hands all over you."

"Leave me alone!" I went downstairs and slammed my bedroom door, praying we didn't wake up my siblings. Mom burst into my room. I guessed the fight wasn't over.

"That black guy is only going to hurt you. Watch! He'll give you something or cheat on you or beat the shit out of you. That's what those guys do."

I wondered where the hell Pat was at that point. "Shut up, Mom. You don't know what you're talking about. Just get out."

After a few more rantings about what a slut I was, I called her a bigot and shoved her out of my room. She toppled over into the kids' toy box and started crying. Then Pat came downstairs. We looked at each other. He looked at my mom. I slammed my door.

The next week I started looking for my own apartment. I found a really nice one-bedroom apartment in a building on the opposite side of the city. Perfect. The rent was a bit on the high side but my job – the one I left Bassey's Pharmacy for – paid me very well, so I could afford it. All the utilities were included, it had air conditioning, a pool and the bus dropped me off right in front of my building.

Grandma and Grandpa were so proud. They even helped me furnish it, which pissed Mom off. I'm not sure whether it was because I wouldn't let her help, or that they were helping me again without my asking them to. I didn't really care. Grandpa gave me a beautiful antique lamp that had a gorgeous blown glass feature that went around the light bulb part. It broke in his basement, but he went garage sale shopping until he found a lamp that had a similar part – just for me!

When I first moved in, they came over to help me arrange my apartment.

"Look at my Tami Whammi in her own place," Grandma said. "What a big girl you've become."

Grandpa put a chair he'd brought from his basement by my balcony doors. "We're so proud of you, Dumplin'. This is quite a fancy place!"

Grandma gave me my own sewing basket, some pictures, and a few dishes. Before they left, Grandma hugged me. "You'll be just fine. We know it."

Grandpa put his hands on my shoulders. "Stay in touch. You are really doing great things." Then he pulled me to his chest.

Things were going so well for me at that point that I wondered how long it would last. Then the first shoe fell. Mark mentioned his other girl-friend had returned from school.

"Don't be so surprised," he said. "You always knew I was sort of seeing this girl. We just said we could see other people. You were fine with it..."

"That's because she wasn't here," I said, hearing how awful that sounded. Yes, I was "the other woman." But I was tired of the title. I gave him an ultimatum: choose her or me. He couldn't make up his mind, so I made it up for him and dumped him.

Shortly after that, the other shoe fell. One morning in the shower, I felt tiny bumps all over my genitals. Now, I was pretty versed in sex, but not with STDs. I thought being on The Pill would protect me from the scariest thing that could happen – getting pregnant. I was wrong.

It turned out that Mark gave me genital warts. And because I ignored the problem for so long before going to a doctor, they spread far and became quite severe. It took over a year of treatments where they burned them off with a dark brown, acid-like medicine. The treatments stung so much I cried at every session, gripping the paper covering on the examination table. The pain lasted for weeks, from one appointment to the next. I cursed Mark every time and hoped he suffered more than I.

It didn't end there. Even after all the burning, the pain, and getting rid of the warts, I still felt sick. In fact, I was having severe pain in my abdomen – sort of like period cramps, multiplied. After a few months of enduring that, I went back to the doctor. I had a pap test, which was so excruciating, I almost threw up in the middle of her examination.

A few days later, my doctor called me. "Tami. I need you to come into the clinic as soon as you can. We have the results of your pap test and, well, I really need to talk to you about them. Can you come in today?"

I felt the blood drain out of my face. My stomach twitched. I decided to go to the clinic alone and say nothing to my mom. I'd already endured enough "I told you so" from her about the STD and all my treatments. The entire bus ride to the clinic, I chewed the inside of my lip, trying not to cry. *What the hell was it now? More warts? They'd missed some and now they're back again? Something worse? God, what could be worse than going through all of that again?*

The clinic receptionist led me directly to my doctor's office. By that point I was so freaked out I just wanted her to spill it already.

"Okay, I'm here," I said when she opened the door. "What is it? More warts?"

The doctor sat on the desk in front of me and put her hand on my shoulder. "No, I'm afraid it's much worse. You have cancerous cells on your cervix. And it's actually quite far advanced. I don't think we'll need to remove the cervix but we need to get you in for laser surgery as soon as possible before it spreads further."

My body went cold. She said the odds were good I'd be fine after the surgery. She gave me statistics and told me the likely source was the HPV virus from the form of genital warts I had contracted. I had no idea how to feel. I should have been scared or worried or pissed off or... something. But I was so shocked I didn't know what to feel first.

Surgery was scheduled for the next month. I had to tell my mom because I needed someone who could drive me to the hospital and take me back home.

A few days beforehand, I called her. We were not a family who led up to bad news – we just napalmed them with it. After a minute of small talk, I came right out with it. "Mom, I need you to drive me to the hospital on Thursday. I found out a couple of weeks ago that I have cervical cancer and I need surgery. They won't do it unless I have someone to pick me up. If you can't do it..."

"No, I'll take you," she said. "I'll just rearrange my students."

Oddly, there was no "I told you so," no lectures, no rants. She picked me up for my 8:00

a.m. surgery, and we never spoke the entire drive. We went to the emergency doors of the Women's Clinic at St. Boniface Hospital. As we walked down the long, narrow hallway, my heart pounded so hard I thought I was going to pass out.

We finally made it to a room with a small reception area. Two other young girls, one with a guy, the other with a female friend, sat in beige faux-leather chairs waiting for their names to be called. I didn't have to wait very long. My mom insisted on coming in with me.

"Why don't you wait out here?" I asked. "I was told it wouldn't be very long."

She ignored me and spoke to the nurse guiding us to the pre-surgery room. "I'm her mother. She's a bit nervous about the whole thing."

I rolled my eyes.

The nurse cleared her throat and held back a curtain to our room, saying, "Take all your clothes off except your bra and socks. Your gown and robe are over there. And be sure to take off any jewelry you have on. I'll be back in a few minutes to take you in to Dr. Manning."

Mom still stayed there. "Look, I think I can undress myself and get ready, Mom. Can you please just wait in the front?"

"Don't be silly, Tam," she said, trying to help me with my sweatshirt. "I'm your mother. I've seen it all before..."

"Mom, stop it!"

We stared at each other while she held onto my sweatshirt and I gripped her hands. Her eyes rimmed with tears.

She wasn't there when I was abused, or when I went to have my stomach pumped, or just about any other serious thing of my experience. But she was there at that moment. I relaxed my hands and smiled weakly. She rubbed my arm then ducked out of the curtain while I undressed.

The place was so cold. My skin turned purple the second I took my shirt off. I put the stiff gown and robe on and told my mom she could come back in.

As she came in, so did the nurse. "It's time to go," she said. "Mom, you can wait here, if you'd like. No one else is allowed in the surgery room with the patient."

Mom walked over to my pile of clothes and started folding them. "It's fine. I'll wait in here. It's fine..."

Hugging my robe tightly against me, I followed the nurse down a series of short hallways. The surgery room was as small as the front area. There was an examination table, a tray with different tools and a big-screen television that I assumed was for the surgery, not watching the soaps.

"Lie down here and scoot down until your bum is at the edge. Great! Now we'll just push this gown up and put your feet into these stirrups. There ya go, my Dear. Okay, we'll just cover you up, and Dr. Manning should be here in few moments. Don't worry. Everything will be okay."

With that, the nurse squeezed my hand and left. I stared at the ceiling. The fluorescent lights buzzed softly. Someone coughed out in the waiting area. My eyes welled up.

God, why is this happening? I don't understand. You let some pervert have sex with me without my permission. Some stupid guy puts his hands all over me without my permission. I choose to have sex with this one guy and I keep getting punished over and over.

Laying there on that table, with my legs spread open, nothing shielding me but some paper-like blanket, I felt more vulnerable than I had when Edward raped me. But now, there was no innocence left to take. Warm streaks ran down the sides of my face.

Dr. Manning finally came in the room. I actually laughed out loud, sniffing away my tears. He looked exactly like Waiter Cam, the guy that waited on us at my tenth birthday. The doctor had shorter hair, no tan, and his shirt had a few extra buttons done up. "Hi there, Tami. I'm Dr. Manning."

He explained to me how the surgery would go: He'd freeze my cervix then literally burn away the cancer with this laser that looked like a long, skinny flashlight. He said I could watch the entire procedure on the television, if I wanted to. I kept my eyes closed the whole time.

It wasn't supposed to hurt, but putting the initial clamp thing in so he could get to my cervix hurt so much he called the nurse in to hold my body still. It was supposed to take only about half an hour but it took over an hour (that may have been due to the fact he had to re-freeze me twice because it didn't "take" the first couple of times). There wasn't supposed to be much bleeding but there was – a lot.

After the surgery, the nurse helped me walk back to my room. Mom wasn't there. I guessed she went for a walk since it took so long.

"Lay here for a little while, Baby Girl," the nurse said. "Dr. Manning won't release you until you can walk a little more steadily, okay? Here's a warm blanket. Just rest."

I lay on my side in the fetal position. My legs felt like I'd been horseback riding for hours, and the freezing was starting to wear off. There had been some cancer on the inside of my cervix so I was warned there would be cramping as my cervix closed back up. They weren't kidding! I wondered whether he used a machete down there. Then my mom peeked through the curtain. "Hey there! All done?"

I was actually happy to see her. "Yeah. Just have to stay here until I'm released."

She sat in a chair shoved right next to my cot, then reached up and held my hand. For some reason, it was okay. After about half an hour, the nurse checked my bleeding and said I could get dressed and go. I walked to the car like a woman who'd just given birth. She opened the door for me and helped me in. Then as Mom walked around the back of the car to her door, I saw it: The brown bag from the liquor store. It was tucked in the back seat under the driver's seat. I snuck a quick peek and saw a magnum of wine that had about a fourth of it missing. *So she'd gone to the Liquor Commission when I came out of surgery.*

I sighed deeply and shook my head. I don't know why I was so disappointed. It isn't like it never happened before. But I thought that maybe, just maybe, for something like this...

The car ride home was pretty quiet. Mom tried striking up a conversation, but I wasn't interested. I just flipped stations on the radio and stared out the window. She walked me up to my apartment. I said, "Thanks, Mom. I appreciate your help but you can go now."

"But Dr. Manning said..."

"I know what he said. My friend Karl is going to stay with me."

"What, that new black boyfriend of yours? Haven't you learned anything?"

I gingerly sat down on my futon. "Plenty. That's why I asked Karl to stay with me."

She crossed her arms. "I am your mother. You aren't letting some boy *du jour* stay with you. You need me."

"No, I don't. Thank you for taking me and for bringing me home, but you aren't staying with me. I need to be calm and that's not going to happen with you here."

Her lip quivered. "Why are you doing this?"

"Because I saw the L.C. bag in the car. If you couldn't handle it, you should have told me. I would have asked Susan or Colleen to come with me."

She stomped over to the door, grabbed her purse from the table and slammed the door behind her. She didn't even call to see if I was okay. But Cam said she didn't come home until the middle of the night, and was so drunk she passed out in the hallway on her way to the bathroom, hitting her head so hard on the way down she dented the wall.

I cried.

The month after my surgery, I lost my job from needing too much time off to recover. Mom offered to let me move back home, but she never let me forget how much she "helped" me.

Cam moved in and out of the house several times, alternately living with his best friend, Robin, or one of his other friends. It would be many years before Cam sought help for his anger and his living nightmares. Heather and Ian were getting older and it was becoming more difficult to shield them.

One night I babysat the kids so Mom and Pat could go to a Christmas party. Heather, all of six, and I looked out of her bedroom window tattooed with frost and ice. We had just enough space to see the driveway. They hadn't come home by bedtime and Heather couldn't sleep until she heard their car. *A ghost from my own past.* I asked Heather what was wrong. She didn't speak for several minutes. Then she said, "Mom's probably drunk."

My heart sank. She was just like me so many years before. Her innocence taken away at such a young age. So unfair. Because Mom had used booze for so many years as a coping mechanism, drinking became a habit. Now we couldn't tell whether her behavior was from drinking or her illness.

That frosty night, with Heather asleep in my lap, I asked God again to take my mother.

"Please," I begged. *"Why would you keep her down here? She obviously doesn't want to be here. Please put her, and us, out of misery. Why do you keep putting us through this?"*

What I didn't realize is, she still needed to be there. We all needed each other to get through the next couple of chapters of our lives. And they proved to be the most difficult.

There were more and more incidents which became increasingly more difficult to recover from. Each time something happened, my heart hardened to her just a little bit more, and it made it difficult to forgive her. Just when the ability to forgive came, she fell off the wagon again. I couldn't deal with it. It ate away at me, literally. At eighteen, I was diagnosed with a stomach ulcer.

I had to swallow these awful fluorescent orange horse pills four times a day to heal my stomach lining. Grandpa was on the same medication. He wasn't very happy that his granddaughter, not even twenty, was being treated for an ulcer. He noticed bruises, bite marks and other markings on me, Mom and Cam. He thought they were from Pat.

Grandpa drove me home after a teatime visit with Grandma and pulled the car over halfway home.

"Does he hit you?" he asked, staring straight ahead.

"Pat?" I was seriously surprised. "No, Grandpa. Pat isn't the one who hits me. He's never laid a hand on me. I swear."

Grandpa sat quietly for several minutes, tears rimming his eyes. I undid my seatbelt and threw my arm across his shrunken frame. He hugged my arm, patting it, then put his stubbly cheek on the top of my head. We said nothing.

A few days after that, Grandpa called my mom, saying Grandma was back in the hospital again and we needed to get there as soon as possible. Pat stayed with the kids while the rest of us went to the hospital. I went into Grandma's room while Mom and Cam went to the family meeting down the hall. It was serious.

This time Grandma was tested for every neurological test available at the time, and the results weren't good: Alzheimer's. It was fairly advanced. I watched Grandma from the doorway of her hospital room. She sat on her bed, her legs dangling over the side. She threw bits of her food on the floor and searched desperately around.

"Coco," she whispered loudly. "Coco, come here, pup. Here's some treats for you. Just don't tell Dad."

I put my hand over my mouth, holding back tears. Coco, our beloved terri-poo, had been put to sleep several years earlier. Grandma saw me and waved me in. I bent down to give her a hug and she clung to me so deeply my ribs hurt. As she spoke, her breath moved through my hair.

"I know what's happening to me, you know. Everyone around here tiptoes around it, but I know. I forget things. I forget faces – even my own family sometimes. I hate it."

I didn't know what to say. I pulled back to look at her. She put her hand on the side of my face and continued. "One day, I may not be able to say this to you, so you just listen. I am proud of who you've become and where you're going. Don't you let anyone make you feel small, you hear me? You're a lot like me, Dumplin', and I'll be watching you. Even when I won't be able to look at you and see you anymore, please know these times will be tucked away in the corners of my mind. Those are the memories I'll take with me. And that's how I want you to remember me."

I cried and buried my face in her chest. She stroked my hair and whispered, "You've always been my favorite, Dumplin'. And I'll never leave you. Not entirely."

Grandma made it through Christmas, but deteriorated rapidly after that. Then she was gone. The source of strength in our family – the main reason we stayed civil to each other – was gone.

As messed up as our family was, we were all there for one another. We were able to put everything aside and provide comfort to one another. But once Grandma left us, the glue that held the rest of us together unstuck. Everyone went their own way. I'm sure Grandma looked down on us from Heaven with heaviness in her heart.

I felt nothing. Not when I found out, not when we made funeral arrangements, and not at her funeral. I was numb. I listened to Grandma's heartfelt eulogy, prepared by our minister. I heard the choir sing, but I still felt nothing. What was wrong with me? One of the most important people in my life was gone, forever, and I couldn't let my feelings surface. I looked up at the familiar stained-glass window. My eyes burned.

There He was again – looking down at me. The rain outside made His eyes darker than usual. I saw drops of precipitation clinging to his eyes then slowly slip down.

You should cry, I thought, watching Him. *How could you take her away from me?*

I managed to block out the entire funeral service. Afterward, the congregation was invited to celebrate Grandma's life in the Conservatory. I sat on a cold, metal folding chair as everyone moved in slow motion around me. People wished me well, said they would miss Grandma, that she was a good woman. I already knew all of that. All I could think of was our conversation when she could still remember me: "You've always been my favorite, Dumplin'. And I'll never leave you."

Suddenly, a slight figure inched toward me. The rain had stopped, and the morning light shone behind her, illuminating her blonde hair. She held her arms out to me as tears streamed down her face: Susan.

She enveloped me in her arms and whispered, "Oh, Tam. I'm so sorry." That's all she had to say. People continued walking around us as we hugged. Letting go at last, I cried.

Grandma always loved Susan.

Chapter Eleven

The Last Straw

Death is not the greatest of evils; it
is worse to want to die and not be
able to.
~ Sophocles (495-405 B.C.E.)

Grandma's death had a huge impact on my
family and me. Each of us reacted to it a different way. I buried my feelings as I always did. I
partied and drank – often.

Grandpa – my pillar of strength – was crushed.
The woman he devoted half his life to was gone,
and with her went part of himself. Every time he
came for a visit he broke into tears. Seeing
Grandpa like that was even more devastating
than Grandma's death, because he was forced
to go on. It was as though he didn't know how.

He had to sell his house, which meant going
through, giving away, and packing up all of the
possessions he and Grandma collected together.

How difficult that must have been for him. Grandma never prepared a will – she felt there would always be a time for such annoying things – so he didn't know what to do with her things. Therefore, most of the furnishings, china, and knick-knacks were put away in storage until Grandpa could bear to deal with them. The practical furniture and precious items, like Grandma's artwork, went with him to his new apartment. He hated his apartment.

Uncle Craig told me Grandpa was a frequent overnight guest in his spare room in the basement. Grandpa hated it that much. Grandpa was lost without Grandma.

I chose to ignore Grandma's death. In my heart, I knew the day would come when I had to say goodbye to my grandparents, but I didn't want to face it. Not ever.

Even going to her gravesite would have meant I accepted her death. I still had Grandpa – even if it was just for a short time. I knew that, most times, when a person loses their partner of many years, it isn't long before they join them. That thought terrified me. On top of partying, I developed another dangerous coping mechanism.

My eating disorder started with aggressive exercise – for about an hour several times a week – just to get rid of angry feelings. I'd been told it was a great way to get rid of negative thoughts and emotions. Soon I was exercising for two to three hours every day. I did aerobics until my muscles ached, my shins hurt and sweat poured down my body. But I was still "full" of my feelings.

One morning my stomach swirled with the alcohol I drank the night before. No matter what I did, I couldn't get rid of the nausea. One of my girlfriends had a solution and I decided to try it: I made myself throw up. That first time, I only did it for relief. I grabbed my toothbrush and tickled my tonsils. I gagged only once before the contents of my stomach spewed out, leaving me with a calming relief.

I rested my head on the cool porcelain while the toilet sucked the memories, and the feelings that went with them, into its bottomless belly. I felt better. And that was how I got rid of my feelings for the next ten years.

I never did it because I thought I was fat. In fact, I had always fought to keep weight on in the past. But when things got too overwhelming, whenever Mom lost control, when I missed Grandma too much, I bought enough food to feed my entire family and ate it all in one sitting: fried chicken, cookies, ice cream, chips, French fries; it didn't matter what.

I shoveled the food into my mouth faster than I could chew it sometimes. With every bite of food, I attempted to bury a memory, a feeling, or an uncomfortable experience. With my stomach stretched beyond its capacity, I'd take several gulps of pop or water. That's all it took. I'd run to the bathroom and throw it all up.

I threw up – sometimes for several minutes – until nothing was left in my stomach. I threw up until the toilet was full and I was empty. Then I flushed it all away.

The feelings never stayed away for long, though. I think Grandpa knew something was wrong with me. He came over for Thanksgiving dinner that year, the first after Grandma died. Mom, Pat, Heather, Ian, Cam, Grandpa and I all sat around our beautiful mahogany dining table overflowing with a complete turkey dinner and all the trimmings. I remember how sad I felt. In all fairness, my mom did a great job: the food was fabulous, the silverware was polished and shiny, the delicately patterned china was inviting; she even stayed sober. Everything was perfect. But I looked around the table and was over-whelmed with sadness.

For some reason, I knew it would be our last dinner together: Our last "family" dinner with Mom and Pat as a façade couple. The last dinner to which I would accept an invitation. Our last dinner without drinking, fighting or anger, and our last dinner with Grandpa.

Mom served everyone, then said, "Let's try something different this year. Why don't we go around the table and say what we're most thankful for. I'll start. I'm thankful for this bountiful feast and that it didn't burn."

Everyone laughed. It was nice to hear laughter.

Everyone was basically grateful for the same things: family, friends, and happiness. Then it was my turn. I didn't know what to say. All I could think of was what I didn't have: self-control, happiness, and Grandma. I looked at

Grandpa with tears filling his eyes and knew I had to say something positive.

"I'm grateful Grandpa could be here to share Thanksgiving with us and wish he always could be."

Grandpa leaned across his plate, grabbed my bony arm and said, "I'm grateful for health, for laughter and for love. And I'm grateful God gave us these things to share – even if it's just for now."

Then he squeezed my arm and wiped his eyes with the back of his hand.

"Are we gonna eat or what?" Cam said.

More laughter.

Grandpa and I locked eyes. He winked at me.

Cam and I moved in together. I'd lived on my own before and so had Cam, but moving in together seemed like a good decision for both of us: partly to share expenses, partly because we already knew how to live together and partly because Cam was worried about me. I went from "skinny" to "emaciated" within a few months. Our roles were now reversed and he was protecting me. Of all the people who surrounded me, only two people, Cam and my dear friend Colleen, had the courage to confront me about my eating disorder. Cam made sure I was never left alone to throw up and Colleen gave me a picture of my skeletal self in a bikini.

It still wasn't enough to stop my inner torture.

Once, on the way to the bathroom, I passed out in the hallway, cracking my head on the wall as I crumpled to the floor. Cam helped me up, saying, "God, your arms are the same size all the way down. You need to eat, Tam. I can't lose you, too."

Years before, I promised my brother I'd never try taking my own life again. I realized then that I lied.

My mom's desperate search for her birth family was finally successful: she found her birth father, Larry, and her brother, Jamie, living in California. Her birth mother had died several years earlier.

Larry sent her a letter in response to one he received from her investigator saying his daughter was looking for him. This began correspondence back and forth for several months.

I never read any of the letters, but my mom told me that she got a lot of the answers she'd wanted all her life. Larry described how heartbroken he was when she was given away. Apparently, he didn't want to give her up but it wasn't his choice. That's how things were done back then. If the mother wanted to give up the child, the father simply complied.

Larry said his wife – yes, mom's parents were married at the time she was given up – wasn't happy about getting pregnant. She was a workaholic and liked to party. She wouldn't get an abortion but did horrific things to try to miscarry, such as punching herself in the stomach or drinking beyond excess. I have no idea why Larry told my mom those things. It was bad enough for her to know her mother didn't want her in the first place.

I thought it was cool that my mom had found her birth family. I didn't even mind that she wanted to meet them. What made me angry was when she chose to set up a meeting. She invited them to spend Christmas with us.

"Seriously, Mom," I said. "The first Christmas since Grandma dies and you invite strangers to spend the holiday with us?"

"They aren't 'strangers,'" she said, chain-smoking. "They're our family. Don't ruin this for me, Tam. You know I've been waiting for this for a long time."

I softened. "I know, Mom. But Christmas? Can't you meet with them after? Did you think of how we'd feel about this? And what about Grandpa?"

"Grandpa knows," she said, crushing a butt in the ash tray then quickly sparking up another cigarette. "I already told him. He's fine with it."

I was also curious to find out about that side of my history, but her timing just sucked.

"You told him you found your birth family and that you invited them here for Christmas?" I asked. "Won't he be uncomfortable being there with them?"

"Oh, Grandpa won't be coming for Christmas," she said, her tone dripping with bitterness. "He's spending it with his girlfriend, Neta, at Craig's house."

A Christmas without Grandma or Grandpa? *Oh, no. I don't think so.*

"Just ask them to come up after. Please?"

Mom hugged herself and rocked back and forth. "No. I've already invited them. They'll be here a couple of days before Christmas Eve. I'd love for you to be here, but if you can't come, I understand."

I promised to go over on Christmas Day, and Cam spent the night there. Pat picked me up the next day. Everyone was hung over. Not the best first meeting.

Larry was a short, stout man with graying hair and an elfish voice that reminded me of someone from the Land of Oz. Jamie didn't say very much but reminded me a lot of Dustin Hoffman's *Rainman* character: he was a genius but didn't make eye-contact and rocked when he wasn't in the conversation. He looked just like Mom, only taller.

I sat slouched into the couch, my arms crossed across my chest, listening to everyone else chat. After only a few hours, the combination of talking about airplanes and mathematics mixed with Larry and Jamie's Chip-and-Dale voices got too much. I asked Pat to drive me back home. Uncle Craig told me Grandpa was devastated about Mom finding her father and brother. But he understood her need to find them. He told her he hoped she found what she was looking for all these years and wished her a Merry Christmas.

That turned out to be the last Christmas Grandpa would be with us and I spent it without him.

My most feared day came.

It was a humid, overcast June day, depicting the mood. I took my latest beau over to my mom's. I still never dated anyone seriously at that point – new "bar" guy every few months. No commitments, no expectations – just fun.

Mom greeted us at the door. Before I could make introductions, my mom grabbed my shoulders. Her eyes were swollen, she was pale and her voice shook when she spoke. "Grandpa had a stroke."

I later learned that while Grandpa was visiting Neta's cabin, he was walking up the stairs from the dock to the cabin and the stroke was so sudden and powerful that he fell to the ground and struck his head on the cement.

I forgot about my boyfriend and joined Cam and Mom who were headed to the hospital. It was apparent by the way my mom gripped the steering wheel and Cam rambled on, that none of us knew what to expect. We definitely weren't prepared for what we saw when we got there.

Grandpa was in a shared room – the ones where a curtain is pulled between two beds. Mom went in first, followed by Cam, and I trailed behind. There he was – someone who looked like Grandpa, but it couldn't have been him.

The man I always looked to for courage, who was tall, strong and larger than life, lay on a sterile single bed with a thin sheet draped over him. He was writhing in pain. He had an IV in his arm. A catheter snaked under the sheet and various monitors were suction-cupped to his chest, head and fingers. The oxygen tube wrapped around his head into his nose and squashed his normally handsome face.

Grandpa? I thought. *Oh, Grandpa.*

Mom hugged his fragile frame. He'd lost weight just in the few days he'd been in the hospital. He seemed surprised to see her, and I made out of his struggling response, "Jannie." I hadn't heard him call her that in years. Cam squeezed Grandpa's arm, then Grandpa looked up and saw me. Tears flooded his eyes as he forced out, "Oh, Taaa...."

I was terrified.

If Grandpa – the one who gave me inner strength all these years and a reason to live – was like that, how could I be strong for him? I dragged my feet toward him. I maneuvered my arms in and around his tubes and monitoring equipment and hugged him with all my strength. He whimpered.

Usually when I put my head on his chest, he put his large hands over my head and whispered, "Hey there, Tami Whammi." His bear hugs made me lose my breath for a few seconds. Now I was doing that to him.

He tried hugging me back, but I put my hands over his arms and smiled. I walked over to a chair against the opposite wall. I faced away from him and closed my eyes. I took a deep breath and swallowed past the lump in my throat. My mom disappeared from the room to talk to a nurse about his condition. Cam went to the bathroom. Grandpa and I were alone.

The oxygen hissed as it forced air into his lungs, the monitors beeped and sputtered out his heart rate, and his feet rubbed against the rough hospital sheets. Every few minutes, he arched his back, squeezed his eyes tight, gripped the blankets so hard his knuckles turned white and thrashed his feet around. I couldn't look at him like that – in so much pain and unable to speak. I didn't want to.

Then I turned to him.

His arm reached out to me.

"Taaa-meee..." he said, straining to get the words out.

I went to him and put my hand in his palm. It still felt strong. He squeezed and clutched my hand to his chest. He opened his mouth to speak but nothing came out. It was excruciating to see a man so witty and articulate not able to utter a single word. I could see that his mind still worked, but his body was failing him.

I sucked in my breath. "Grandpa, please don't try to speak. It's okay..."

But he squeezed my hand again, thumping it on his chest as if to say, "I need to try."

His face turned red as he tried desperately to speak, "I...ahm...sor...sorry."

The burning in my eyes became harder to control.

"You...be...sssstttt...ssstrong..."

He pressed my hand to his chest then shoved our hands back into my chest, saying, "Aaaa...always...hhhh...hhhere..."

I squeezed my eyes shut, wiping the few tears that managed to escape. I held our hands to my chest until Mom and Cam came back. By then, Grandpa had fallen asleep and I laid his arm by his side.

Mom threw her purse into the chair I had been sitting on and dragged a thin metal chair beside the bed. She lifted Grandpa's arm, tucking it under the sheets. "Was he sleeping the whole time?"

I shook my head.

"Well, what did he say?" she whispered.

I went back to the chair, tossing Mom's purse on the floor. "Nothing, really."

Mom rolled her eyes at me.

Whatever. She didn't need to know what was said. It was our secret – mine and Grandpa's.

That was the last time I saw or spoke to Grandpa. Uncle Craig said that after our visit, Grandpa suffered several mini strokes. He held on for a few more days then let go. I didn't go back to the hospital after that visit. I sat at home for those days in a trance: I hardly ate, I barely slept and I wouldn't speak...to anyone. Then one morning, I felt a huge wave of relief pass through my body.

Cam, who had been back and forth at the hospital all week, came home. His eyes were red and swollen. He rubbed my shoulder gingerly. "Mom wanted to come and tell you, but I told her I needed to be the one. He's gone, Tam. I'm so sorry."

He left me with an encouraging hug. One tear fell defiantly from each eye as I hugged him back.

Grandpa was gone.

The funeral was three days later. Grandpa was cremated. I wore a black sundress with pink and purple flowers on it. Grandpa liked that dress. It hung off my skeletal frame.

After a bit of lunch, Pat, Mom, Cam and I met the rest of our family at the church. We waited in the choir practice room with Uncle Craig and Dorothy, Uncle Rick and Kate, and our cousins, as the church filled with people who wanted to say goodbye to Grandpa.

Nobody in our family spoke.

With everyone seated in the church, the minister came to usher us in. Our family was led to the front pew. I tried to tune out the service.

"...and when I visited Wilf in the hospital, he spoke often of his fond memories of summers at the lake with Tami and Campbell..."

I closed my eyes.

Stop. Please stop.

"...his love for his family was obvious by his support of their endeavors. He especially loved his grandchildren and bragged about their accomplishments to everyone: Tami's music, Campbell's soccer games..."

From high above the choir loft, I felt His eyes on me again, just like at Grandma's funeral. I refused to look this time.

"...and words often used to describe him were '...a perfect gentleman...the last of a dying breed'..."

Then my Auntie Lois sang. Auntie Lois has the voice of angels and a gift to move even the hardest of hearts to tears. Grandpa loved her. She sang "The Lord's Prayer."

As the piano played, my eyes blurred with tears.

No, no, no, no, no...I won't cry. I don't accept this.

Cam gripped my hand and our fingers entwined. With every strong pulsating note, Cam and I gripped a little harder. I finally had the courage to look up behind Auntie Lois.

The stained glass Jesus stared at me.

His eyes were bright this time, because the sun shone behind them. He seemed to reach out to me. My mind filled with such hateful thoughts it took all my inner strength not to run from the church.

Don't look at me like that. I hate you. You took Grandma and Grandpa and now I'm all alone. I'll never forgive you. Ever.

Just like at Grandma's funeral, tea and dainties afterward gave family and friends a time to talk and remember my grandfather. I don't remember much about it. The one comment I do remember was my Uncle Rick telling me, "It's okay to have a bit of weight on you, you know."

My Auntie Lois gave me her phone number. "This must be excruciating for you, my Dear," she said, hugging me. "Keep that phone number and use it if you need me for anything. I wasn't able to do more for you when you were a little girl, but I can help you through this. We need good friends and God in our hearts when we're in pain."

God? I don't think so.

The boyfriend of the month I'd brought to meet my mom got tired of leaving me messages and moved on. What did it matter?

The months that followed Grandpa's funeral were heart-wrenching. My mom was cut out of

Grandpa's will. His words were bitter: "To Janet, I leave nothing. After supporting her over the years, I feel she has been more than compensated for."

Even my uncles were shocked by Grandpa's decision. They tried to be fair, though. They got my mom to choose certain things from his possessions that meant a lot to her and would help her to heal.

Cam stopped talking to that side of our family. My uncles stopped talking to our mother because she started calling them when she was drunk. They tried being fair with her – giving her things neither of my grandparents thought she deserved. But she kept calling them, harassing them and accusing them of stupid things, like brainwashing my Grandpa into hating her.

One phone call got so heated that Uncle Craig said, "Janet, I can't deal with this bullshit any more. We're all tired of it. Don't call here unless you're sober and sane. Enough already!"

Cam was there that time and told Uncle Craig to screw off and hung up on him. I have no idea why. Everyone was mad at each other and no longer felt any need to keep up the façade that we were a loving, happy family. I was caught in the middle and fell into a deep depression.

I didn't want to talk to anyone or be around anyone. I stopped working. I didn't want to get out of bed or get dressed or leave the apartment. When Cam lost his job too, we weren't able to pay our rent, so we had to move back in with Mom and Pat. Their house wasn't big enough for four adults and two growing kids.

And all of us living in the same house only seemed to fuel the old problems.

Soon after Cam and I moved in, Mom had a three-day drinking binge that ended with her taking off to the lake. Cam and Pat had to go find her and force her to come back home. That was, as the saying goes, the final straw for me.

And I needed to find the strength to reach out before I destroyed myself.

PART III:

LOST & FOUND

Chapter Twelve

When A Door Closes,
A Window Opens

Her beautiful hair dropped over me –
like an angel's wing.
~ Charles Dickens (1812–1870)

When Grandpa died, part of me did too. I was going on twenty-five and my life just seemed to stop. Gone was the girl who felt the need to protect, to cover up or pretend. There was no point. Both of my reasons for keeping secrets were dead. But in order to move forward, I had to let that part of me go. And it terrified me.

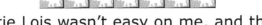

Auntie Lois wasn't easy on me, and the task of saving me wasn't easy on her.

I moved into Auntie Lois' house two months before Christmas.

Mom had been on a week-long drinking binge and took off to the Lake with Heather and Ian. Cam and Pat went to find her. They left me behind, "just in case Mom comes back." That was fine with me. I had no intention of going anyway.

After they left, I sat there for hours in my room, staring at the thirteen-inch television. I flicked through the stations. It didn't matter what was on. I just needed the noise.

I didn't want to be there anymore. I didn't want to keep coming back to that frigging house and being a part of all of that crap anymore. I knew what would happen: Cam and Pat would find Mom. They'd drag her back kicking and screaming (in front of her young children). She'd pass out. When she'd get up the next morning, no one would say one damn word.

My heart pounded in my bony chest and I threw the remote at the television with all my might. It bounced off the top and shot behind the television stand. The TV turned off. I grabbed a package of green garbage bags I'd thrown on the floor earlier. I was going to clean up my room. I didn't know why. It was just something I thought needed to be done right then.

I started ripping the package apart. I cursed, screamed, and yelled at the top of my lungs until the package was torn to shreds and garbage bags were strewn around my room. Then I flopped on my bed, exhausted.

No tears, though. Not a drop.

As I lay there, I looked at the TV stand and saw the scrap of paper with Auntie Lois' phone number. That's when I decided I needed to give Auntie Lois a call.

"Hello? This is Lois speaking," she said after the second ring. She always answered the phone like that.

"Auntie Lois," I said. "Mom is gone again. I... I mean...can I....?"

There was a brief silence. Then Auntie Lois said, "I wondered when you'd finally call me, my Dear. Come. Do you need a ride?"

"I have a ride."

Uncle Craig came over and helped me load the few boxes and garbage bags that contained my precious belongings into his minivan for the short trip across the city to Auntie Lois' house. Part of me felt terrible, as she was newly married and trying to get used to her new role as wife and stepmom, but she insisted.

I loved her for it, but I kept most of my things stuffed in green garbage bags my entire stay – just in case I had to leave again quickly.

My stay was painful for many reasons. First, I revealed everything that happened to Cam and me over our lifetime: the drinking, the abuse, Mom taking off, the sexual abuse, the affairs, my overt behavior – everything. Of course, it didn't spill out all at once. Little pieces of the puzzle were taken out each day – and only as much as I could bring out at a time – as I was ready to talk. Auntie Lois made "us time" where we chatted over a mug of tea. She even bought me a book called *All About Me*, which was sort of like a diary with writing prompts. It was geared to young adults going through trauma like eating disorders, abuse, etc. If anyone else had given it to me, I'd have been pissed off and told them to mind their own business. But Auntie Lois genuinely cared. She knew talking was difficult for me, so she cared enough to give me a tool to help the thoughts, memories and words come. During our "us times" I'd bring out a part of the book I'd worked on to help open the door. When I was ready to talk about things, she never once told me to stop or accused me of lying. She just listened, hugged me, and understood.

There was one part that had the outline of a body and instructions to draw how I saw myself and explain why. That was a tough one.

"So what should we talk about today?" Auntie Lois asked.

I sat with my book in my lap for a few seconds. I was afraid of her reaction since we hadn't spoken about my eating disorder yet – not that it wasn't obvious I struggled with weight issues.

I took a deep breath then opened the book to the body diagram.

"May I peek?" she asked, as she always did.

I stared at the picture before giving it to her. I'd originally drawn big eyes with a line saying I liked my eyes. I'd also drawn long straight hair, big baggy clothes and no smile. Then I scribbled all over it. The only explanation I gave was, "What's there to like?"

Auntie Lois took the book, laying it in her lap, then said, "This makes me so sad, Tami, because when I look at you I see many things I don't just like but love."

She took the pen, drew a line to the eyes I'd drawn and wrote, "Eyes that are so blue they shine. Happiness should be here."

She drew a line to my mouth and wrote, "When this mouth is smiling, her whole face shines. And her laugh is both warm and contagious."

Another line to my arms, "These arms gave the best squeezy hugs I ever got when Tami was wee."

Then she turned to me. "I could write so many good things about you. This...," she said, drawing a circle around the body outline, "...isn't going to seem beautiful to you until you see inside here first. Things need to be cleared out, cleaned up and healthy so that it can be seen on the outside. It will come and I'll help you."

She put her arm around my shoulder and pulled me close. I can't describe the comfort I felt with Auntie Lois in any other way than to say she warmed my insides. I'd never felt that before – but I liked it.

The first few months I was there, Mom called Auntie Lois almost every night – drunk, of course. Auntie Lois told me that my mom accused me of everything from "...using people then dumping them once she got what she wanted," to being "an ungrateful little bitch."

One night, after Auntie Lois had talked to my mom for almost an hour, she called me into her bedroom. As I ascended the stairs, my heart sank to my stomach. I thought, "Great. Another person will side with Mom and not believe me."

I reached the doorway and she waited for me on her bed, her face flushed, her eyes red. She patted beside her on the multi-colored floral print quilt. When I sat, she pulled me to her and rested her chin on the top of my head.

"I spoke with your mother," she said, stroking my hair.

I half expected her to tell me to pack my stuff and get out. "What did she say?"

"She had a lot of things to say," Auntie Lois said. "What she forgot was that I've known her since junior high and everything she was accusing you of, she did herself. Even if you hadn't told me what you've been through, Tami, I'd have known the truth. God reveals what's true even if we don't always see it at first."

A wave of emotion rose in me. It seemed to bring with it all I'd repressed since the day I'd heard my mom tell Grandma she didn't want Cam and me.

In that moment, as I felt Auntie Lois hug me – a person who really believed me, a person so close to God she could be considered an angel – the flood gates opened and I cried. I cried for the little girl I never was. I cried for all the times I hurt but couldn't react. I cried for not having a mother who loved me the way she wanted to. And I cried for losing Grandma and Grandpa. I cried until my body was cold and shaking while Auntie Lois held me and rocked.

When I finally stopped crying and sat up, Auntie Lois tried putting her hand on the side of my face. I turned and squinted my eyes.

"Oh, dear Tami," she said. "I can tell what terrible turmoil you've experienced when a normal gesture of affection – like touching your beautiful face – would cause you to recoil in fear. Not all people are hurtful. Not all people want things from you. Some only want to love you and keep you safe. That's all I want. And that's what God wants."

She turned my face toward her and held it in her hands, a gesture I rejected from most people.

"I'm your Godmother, Tami. It's my job to guide your spirit and enlighten your soul. You don't have to be afraid anymore. From this day on, I'll make sure you'll never ever have to suffer the way you have again. I promise."

I clung to her. For the first time since Grandma pzassed away, I believed my existence mattered. And I allowed someone else to care for and love me.

It felt nice.

Auntie Lois found out about my eating disorder due to an unusual carelessness on my part: I forgot to flush the toilet one day after a purge. Her stepson, whose turn it was to clean the bathroom, discovered my error. He and I had become very close during my stay – like Cam and I used to be – so his concern for me was real.

He burst into my room, the doorknob bouncing off the wall. "Hey. You not feeling good?"

I had been lying down, but bolted up after the crash. "I'm okay," I said, breathing hard to calm my racing heart. "You scared the crap out of me!"

"I asked you if you're sick or something. There's puke in the toilet."

I felt my face get hot. "Yeah. I mean no, I'm not feeling good. Must have been something I ate for breakfast."

"Uh-huh," he said, stuffing his hands into his back pockets. "You don't exactly eat very much with all of us. And you seem not to feel well a lot. Maybe you need to gain some weight."

He knew. "Yeah, I was thinking I should gain about five pounds or so."

"Five?" he said, laughing. "You know, Tami, I...never mind. I hope you feel better."

Then he left my room as charismatically as he'd entered it. And, as I found out later on, he went straight upstairs and told Auntie Lois. My long-kept secret was revealed. Part of me was relieved. It had become a habit I couldn't shake no matter how hard I'd tried, and at that point my weight was a scary 78 pounds! Left to go on, I would have died.

I stayed in my room, dreading my next meeting with Auntie Lois. I kept up the charade of not feeling well by skipping dinner and staying in my room. Around ten o'clock, when I thought everyone had gone to bed, I sneaked out to have a bowl of cereal. Auntie Lois was sitting in the dining room drinking a cup of tea. A surge of adrenaline exploded in my stomach.

"Tami," she said, stirring her drink. "Can you come in here for a moment?"

I walked through the kitchen to the dining room and sat across from her at the table.

"If you hadn't come in for your nightly cereal, I was going to come to check in on you before I went to bed. I hear you weren't feeling well today."

I slumped in the chair, leaning my head against the back. "No."

She blew into her cup, then sipped. "Something you want to talk about?"

Oh c'mon! Seriously? Wasn't there a rule that God made about playing mind games with your Godchildren?

I still didn't answer.

She put her cup down. "How long have you been doing this to yourself, Tami?"

"Too long..." I whispered.

She got up and pulled out the chair beside me. "I'm very concerned for you, Tami. We need to nourish you, inside and out. That means you need to talk to someone to address what's making you hurt yourself. Then we need to find a way to re-teach you to eat."

I agreed to let Auntie Lois make me an appointment to see a counsellor at the Christian Counselling Clinic she went to. I connected with a counsellor named Mary and started seeing her once a week. Not only did I relearn how to eat, I also started talking about my past. Both Auntie Lois and Uncle Craig came to several sessions with me to give some extra insight into my situation. After all, they both grew up with my mom and could give details from the past that may have helped. Each of us kept secrets for Mom – even stuff I didn't know about. In one session with Uncle Craig, he revealed that he'd done a lot of the same things I'd been doing to protect my mom: He covered for her when she took off; he lied to my grandparents about Mom's drinking (e.g., when she stole booze from Grandpa's stash); and he cleaned up her messes. When he got older and moved out of the house, he listened to her drunken rants over the telephone.

"I used to take the heat from our parents for what she did," he said. "You know, the drinking and stuff. I thought it was better for me to admit it and cover for her."

The counselor nodded, then asked, "What made this woman so powerful that she could do whatever she wanted while you all picked up the pieces?"

Neither of us knew how to answer her question. She was right, though. My mom seemed to expect a net to be tossed out for her no matter what she did. That was powerful! Why the hell were we doing that?

I'll remember what the counselor said in response to our silence for the rest of my life. She leaned to me and said, "This is what I call the 'White Elephant.' The story goes that a White Elephant is a precious life but very difficult to care for. It seems like the bigger it gets the more difficult it is to care for. And that White Elephant seems to know not only that it is precious, but also that everyone will care for it no matter what it stomps on, bumps into, knocks over or hurts – including those who care for it. If allowed to, caring for it becomes all-consuming until there's nothing left. You need to teach that elephant to care for itself before she crushes you."

After the counselor finished speaking, Uncle Craig took his glasses off and wiped his eyes. I'd never seen him cry before then.

Then Auntie Lois came to one of my sessions where we talked about where my eating disorder may have stemmed from and how I was using it to regain power of my own.

"Janet has a unique gift of getting just about anyone to do what she wants," Auntie Lois said. "She's been that way as long as I've known her. When you aren't willing to go along with her, she gets persistent, then forceful – almost rude. And if she's drinking at the same time, well, it's just a recipe for disaster. I've walked out on her many times. Now we barely speak. I think that sort of chaos and complete focus on her mom's wants – not even needs – may have been a part of what drove Tami to where she is now."

I don't think I was ready for counseling at that point. But I did get some comfort hearing that the things with Mom, like her mood swings and her drinking, weren't just something I saw. Everyone seemed to see it. So why the hell wasn't anyone doing anything about it? That was one question I still hadn't been given the answer to. No one seemed to want to answer it for me.

I started going to church again while I stayed with Auntie Lois. She invited me to come but there was never any pressure to go. I wanted to, but I don't think I was ready for that, either. The first few times, I sat with Auntie Lois' sister and

brother while she sang in the choir. It felt –
strange. Then one Sunday I let my mind wander
too much while the minister did his sermon. I
noticed the stained glass window above the
choir. It was different than the one at the church
I grew up in, but He was still there – staring at
me. Then I thought about being a kid in church,
sitting between Grandpa and Grandma.

Then the stupid organist started playing my
grandfather's favorite hymn: "Thine Is The Glory."
My eyes got hot. A sharp pain stabbed me in the
chest. I wanted to run out of the church. I
started breathing so fast I thought I was going
to pass out. But I didn't.

I stood up with my hymn book open and I
sang. I stared right at him and sang, choking
back the tears that threatened to fall.

*See? I'm just fine. I don't need You. And me
being here doesn't change anything.*

I didn't go back to Auntie Lois' church after
that. I wasn't ready. It was too hard. I still
prayed and was very spiritual, but being in
church – in His house – hurt too much. I also
didn't go back to the counselor I'd been seeing
because she was a Christian counselor and half
of being helped by her was to "accept Jesus as
my Savior." At that point, I just wasn't ready to
have another person – or being – love me. Until
that point, everyone who said they loved me
abused me, left me, or died. I couldn't let God
or Jesus or Joe Blow into my heart until I was
able to get rid of all of the pain I'd hung onto so
tightly. There was no room.

Christmas came and went. Auntie Lois and Uncle Craig kept close tabs on me. They phoned each other daily to "check in" with how I was doing, if I was eating and staying active, and how my moods were. I guess they were worried that the first Christmas without either of my grandparents would be so overwhelming for me I'd cash it all in. I was in pain, but not so weak I avoided all the decorating, baking and celebratory festivities. Auntie Lois invited me to participate in her Christmas Dinner festivities. I agreed.

Her mother remembered me from when I was a child and was thrilled to have me there. I loved her because she was an older version of Auntie Lois: same personality, same talents, same infectious laugh. She walked in the door, approached me with her arms open wide, saying, "Tami! Oh my goodness! It's wonderful to see you!"

She hugged me with so much force she actually squeezed the air from my lungs. Then she pulled me away from her so she could scan my frame. I thought the red-and-black velour swing top and black tights might have hidden my scrawny frame – not from Auntie Lois' mom.

"My GOD you're lanky," she said. "Isn't she lanky, Loie? Just like Jeannie was. Ugh. To only have that kind of body!"

Auntie Jeannie was my dad's sister. As it was revealed over the course of the evening – and something I already knew years ago from reading Mom's diary – my dad was actually dating Auntie Lois' older sister, Marcie, when he met my mom. I have no idea what happened, and no one was ever willing to divulge the entire truth, but I had my guesses.

Despite everything – the losses, the heartache – I had a great Christmas. I was so fortunate to have been there at that time. I needed to be there. I wasn't a blood relative, but I felt more a part of a family than I had since I was a little girl snuggling up with Grandpa in front of the fire listening to Bing Crosby singing "White Christmas." I was so blessed and, in a way, I think I was meant to be there. I had to learn that love didn't always have to hurt. That it was okay to lean on people once in a while, to reach out and to accept help when needed.

It was all good.

In March of 1995, I waffled for weeks about whether I should contact my dad. I'd been thinking about him a lot, and Auntie Lois and Uncle Craig thought I should try re-connecting with him after everything that had been going on. The whole idea felt weird to me. I'd only ever contacted him when I needed money. But he deserved more than that. He deserved the chance to have his side heard – to be understood. I blamed him for too long. It was time for both of us to come clean and talk about our mutual pain. I called him.

It took me many tries before finally letting the phone ring through. I hoped the hang ups wouldn't show up on the long distance charges since Dad had been transferred to Edmonton.

Finally, a cheery female voice picked up, "Hello?" It was my stepmom, Robin.

I chatted with her for a few minutes, before she passed the phone to my dad. He sounded the same. I told him about Grandma and Grandpa, what had been going on, and even that I'd been in counseling. I probably babbled on forever, but he listened. Finally after my throwing everything out there, he asked, "What can I do for you?"

"Would it be okay for me to come out there for awhile? You know, not forever. Just to figure things out, get back on track and, maybe, get to know each other?"

"Sure," he said without hesitation. "I'll have to talk to Rob about it because we have the kids now, but I'm sure it will be fine. We all need help to get through rough times."

I said I'd call him in a couple of days and that was it. Before deciding for sure whether to go, though, I needed to have a one-on-one with Uncle Craig. Since I had moved in with Auntie Lois, he'd become my closest confidant, ally, and almost-big-brother. This was great timing since Cam chose to side with Mom and cut ties with me.

Craig was house-sitting a friend's condo. I told him I needed to have one of our chats like we used to have when I was a kid. He picked me up at Auntie Lois' and brought me to the condo. He made us both a cup of tea, wrapped himself in a blanket (like me, he always felt cold), folded his hands in his lap and said, "Okay. I'm ready. Spill. What's up?"

"I called Dad yesterday," I said, flicking the string on my tea bag.

"Yeah?"

"I'm thinking of going out there. I need to figure out stuff. Maybe he can give me answers I don't have."

Uncle Craig nodded. "I think it's a good idea. I always liked your dad. He was a great guy even if Grandma had her knickers in a knot about Janet getting knocked up by an Army guy."

We laughed.

Uncle Craig got serious again. "Are you up to it, though?"

I wrapped my hands around my steaming mug of tea. The cold weather had never been a friend of mine, but even less so at only 85 pounds (and I'd gained weight at that point). "Will there ever be a good time?"

He gave me a half smile. "I guess not. Okay, then. I think it's a great idea. I have business in Edmonton, and I could be there during your first week. It might help ease you into things, if that's okay."

"Listen. I have to tell you something – thanks."

He frowned. "For what?"

I sighed, staring into my cup. "For being there. For believing me. For everything. You know..."

He shook his head. "I haven't done that much. I haven't done enough. I walked away for a while, you know, to get my head back on straight. 'Being there' for your mom was draining. But I forgot that walking away from her meant leaving you there..."

"What would you have done? Taken us away from her? Have her committed? I doubt you would have done anything differently. No one was strong enough."

He nodded. "You're pretty strong, kiddo."

"Grandma and Grandpa both told me they were sorry before they died, you know. I don't think they really knew what was going on."

"If they had, Grandpa would have taken you guys away from her."

I shook my head. "No, he wouldn't. It would have made things too easy for her. That's what she wanted."

We sat in silence for a few minutes. Then I said, "I'm going. I need to figure out a few things so I can get better."

Uncle Craig tapped my knees. "I think it's a great idea."

So, once again, I packed up all my belongings, which Uncle Craig helped me prepare, and sent them ahead to Edmonton. I caught up with them a few days later, but before I left, Uncle Craig and I went to Grandpa and Grandma's gravesite. I still wasn't ready, but I needed to try.

We stood there, in shin-high snow. I still felt empty and unwilling to accept that they were both gone. And I couldn't make eye contact with the headstone.

"I miss them so much, Tam," Uncle Craig sniffed as he rested his mitted hand on my frail shoulder. I always liked standing in front of Uncle Craig because I felt so safe snuggled into his six-foot-four frame. He stooped down, sweeping snow from the base of the gravestone.

He wore a woolen toque, covering his ever-growing bald spot. His glasses fogged as his tears flowed freely. I wished I could do the same.

When he stood up, he reached out to me. I clasped his mitt in mine and said, "Me, too."

We didn't speak for several minutes. Uncle Craig stared at the headstone and I kept my eyes on the ground in front of it, still unable to face them. Then he guided me to his minivan and drove me to the airport. The real journey to my past began.

Chapter Thirteen

The Seeds Get Carried

Somewhere along the line, I started
hurting the people I care most about,
and I can't figure out how to stop.
~ Dan Scott (fictional character)

The first weekend with my dad and his family
was strange. Uncomfortable. To be fair, we were
essentially strangers. None of us knew how to
act, and the silences were painful. We were so
different and yet...so much the same.

Fortunately, Uncle Craig had business in
Edmonton that first weekend so he made the
first few days easier. He took me out for supper,
toured me around West Edmonton Mall – or at
least part of it – then joined me at Dad's for
cocktails the night before he had to return to
Winnipeg.

It was a Sunday. Robin and Kahla were
already in bed, and Ryan fell asleep in my lap –

too excited that his big sister, whom he'd only known from photographs, was staying with him for a while. Dad let him stay up to cuddle with me. With Dad on one side of me, Uncle Craig on the other – each of them with a full glass of Dad's homemade white wine – and beautiful Ryan asleep in my lap, I knew the time was right.

"Your Mom did a great job raising you all by herself," Dad said, fingering his wine glass stem. He'd said this several times since my arrival, but I chose to ignore it. Dad has often accused Cam and me of making inaccurate statements about our past from "innocent naiveté." He was equally naïve about our upbringing.

"Stop giving her credit she doesn't deserve," I said.

His brow furrowed. "What do you mean?"

Uncle Craig put his hand on my leg. I took a breath and tried again. "I mean, Mom didn't raise us by herself. Technically she didn't raise us at all. We raised ourselves. Without Grandma and Grandpa, we wouldn't have made it."

I told Dad everything: the abuse, the "vacations," Mom's manic behavior, the drinking. While I spoke he nodded occasionally – he understood; he'd gone through it all, too. Then he told me his side: the cheating, the fighting, their excruciating breakup, his staying away because it was just easier.

For who?

"I respected Wilf tremendously," Dad said. "He was always kind to me. Your Uncle Craig here, too – very fair. But your Grandma didn't like Army people. I guess she didn't trust them or something. And she made it quite clear she didn't want me near you kids. Or Janet. I thought it was easier on everyone, especially you kids, if I let them take over. But it was hard. When your Mom got on the plane in B.C. with you guys... when I came to visit you and you didn't recognize me...it hurt."

Part of me understood. Still, if I had been in his shoes, come hell or high water, nothing would have kept me from my children. And I would *never* have left them with someone as unstable as my mother. Knowing Dad and his family just... stepped aside...and let Mom take us – no matter what they were up against – was something I had trouble accepting.

I knew Dad did what he thought was right. He was too young. But if he saw signs of the sort of parent our mother could be – drunk during the day, manic episodes where she took off leaving me crying in my crib – why did he let her take us?

Several questions were still left unanswered: Did he and his family fight for us? Did they think about us? Why didn't they come and see us? Or make sure we were okay? I never got the complete answers to these questions. Dad's family was terribly hurt and bitter about the divorce and losing Cam and me. Some of them still won't talk about it. But at least I knew Dad wanted us – there were just forces that made him believe he wasn't good enough. I got that part.

Uncle Craig liked my dad, too. And he understood how powerful Grandma could be when it came to her kids and grandkids. I didn't feel abandoned anymore. And I wasn't angry with Dad. But he had to know one thing.

"You are my father, but you aren't my dad," I said, as I stroked Ryan's angelic bleach-white tresses. "Grandpa was my dad. He was there for me all those years whenever I needed him. No, he didn't know what really happened in our house, but he was there for me. He came to my school plays, my choir performances, all of my piano recitals; he took care of us when things got out of hand; he provided for us when Mom wasn't able to. He taught me what love was and that I was worthy of it."

I know some of Dad's family accused me of putting my grandparents on a pedestal. I didn't. They were human and made mistakes. And they weren't absolved from blame in letting things go with my mom. But Grandma and Grandpa were there. I hurt Dad. I didn't mean to; I just didn't want him to think more would come out of our reunion than could. I think he wanted me to know the same thing.

I looked into his eyes. For a brief moment, I understood the half of myself I always wondered about: my sarcastic sense of humor, the "Laird nose," my impatience, my need for order.

"We'll never have a true 'daughter/father' relationship," I said softly. "You missed out on that, and we can never go back. But we can go from here forward and get to know one another. I want, at the very least, to become friends."

He agreed. Then he got up and disappeared into his bedroom. When he came back, he held a small, white box and placed it in my hand.

Inside was his wedding band nestled within several layers of cotton. "You kept this?" I asked. "All of these years?"

Dad swigged the rest of his wine. "I don't know why. It was to remind me that no matter what else went wrong, I still had two things out there I did right: you and Cam. I wanted you to have it."

Uncle Craig said that keeping the ring showed what sort of person Dad was. It showed he had compassion others weren't allowed to see, regrets he didn't talk about, and a past too painful to acknowledge. Just like me.

Dad and I bonded that night. And regardless of the events that happened later, I held a deep respect for my father. He and I will forever share a common emotion: we both tried and failed to make it work with my mom.

Things went well for me in Edmonton at first: I had two jobs, saved some money and felt good about myself. Maybe I was being good because I just wanted to please my dad. I missed someone being proud of me. But I don't think Dad knew how to act with me, and there were times I knew he saw Mom in my face. It kept him at bay with his affection. Then, maybe because we were so opposite – or too much alike? – small things revealed what it would have been like to be his live-in daughter.

He forgot my 26th birthday because he was too drunk to make it home. He decided to have a few beers with his buddies at the mess. Robin had everything ready – dinner, balloons, cake –

but he never showed up. It honestly didn't even phase me. After all, it wasn't the first birthday he and I didn't get to spend together.

The next day he went out early and came home after breakfast with a tiny jewelry box: diamond earrings. It's not that I didn't like the gift; it just felt all too familiar.

Dad liked to entertain. He was always the host with the most. Unfortunately, his humor could be dark and very sarcastic when he'd had a few drinks, almost the style of Dennis Leary. And he said hurtful things when he drank – disrespectful things, especially to Robin. The atmosphere often pulled me back to childhood where I had to tiptoe around, not knowing what minute thing would set someone off. It got to the point where I couldn't function unless I drank, too, and I fell off the wagon.

All it took was one person – a person from a bad crowd – to invite me back into the world of sex, drugs and rock and roll. I jumped right on board. I stayed out all night, I spent most of what I earned on alcohol, I slept with people I barely knew, and I just didn't care. Robin tried to tell me Dad cared but he was scared to get hurt.

Hurt? He is afraid I'll hurt him?

Then it hit me: he still saw that little girl who yelled at him and told him to go away. The girl who didn't know who he was and didn't want anything to do with him. We were both doing the same thing: avoiding the loss of someone we loved.

It all came to a head on a weekend Dad, Robin and the kids went on a weekend ski trip.

I stayed behind because I had to work. I decided to allow a few people to come over, but it didn't turn out that way. It was like a scene from *Degrassi Junior High*.

People poured into Dad's house. A lot of them I'd never met before. A scale was set up in the middle of Dad's kitchen table where drug sales were made; some guy smoked crack in the kitchen; people passed joints around on Dad's back steps and threw the ends up in his gutter; a group of people locked themselves in the bathroom "sampling" top-of-the-line something; and people had sex everywhere.

It was out of control. I was out of control. What was I doing? Those were the parties Mom took Cam and me to and I cursed her for including us. I was using Dad's house – his sanctuary – to do the same thing.

"Get out," I screamed at the top of my lungs. "Get out or I'll call the cops!"

For the most part, his house was okay. People stole some booze, left a film of...something I couldn't get off the bathroom mirror, and broke a showerhead in Dad's bathroom, but I was lucky. I should have known better. I wasn't a *Degrassi Junior High* student; I was 26 years old! I was ashamed.

Dad was understandably enraged. But I was certain I couldn't make it on my own. I begged him to allow me to stay. "Please, Dad. Please let me stay. I'll get help. I'll change. I won't hang out with those people anymore..." He stood firm. He kicked me out. I would have done exactly the same thing.

He couldn't even look at me. "I can't have this around my family. I have children I have to protect. And I'm sorry but...I just don't trust you. I want to help you but I can't. I just can't be responsible for my adult children. Not anymore."

I scoffed. "You weren't responsible for your infant children, either."

Ouch!

He walked away from me, saying, "We're still here. Please go."

That was it. I was in Edmonton, basically alone, my one last chance to pull my head out of my butt, and left with only my party friends. I partied with them for a little while, but my health got so bad, I shook when there was no alcohol in my system.

I guess I should have been grateful to Dad because someone finally did for me what nobody did for Mom: I was forced to hit rock bottom. I fell into a sand pit where every time I tried to pull myself out, I slid further backwards. I knew I did it to myself. I was an adult; I couldn't blame my mother for everything I did after I'd removed myself from her web.

My lowest point, the exact moment the light went on for me, was on Christmas Eve. I was alone in my cheap, one-bedroom apartment. I sat with a complete chicken dinner in front of me and I couldn't eat. The meal was thanks to the Edmonton Food Bank. I qualified for assistance – food certificates – because I was on welfare.

There I sat, in my half-empty tiny apartment, with Jimmy Stewart in the background helping an angel get his wings. I was alone. I couldn't afford a telephone. I didn't know how I was going to get groceries once the food certificates were used up. I didn't know how I was going to pay my rent in a few weeks if Welfare cut me off. I had no furniture or any possessions left worth money because I pawned everything.

But...I had a steaming hot piece of chicken breast, lumpy mashed potatoes, mixed vegetables, dark mushroom gravy and a glass of milk. The same meal I'd had every year at Grandma's house. Jimmy Stewart looked up as a tiny bell jingled on his Christmas Tree – the angel got his wings – and I cried.

I needed to go back home and face the demons that waited for me there. Once and for all.

During the time I spent in Edmonton with my dad – and on my own – Cam was in Winnipeg with Mom, Pat, Heather and Ian. I felt guilty about leaving Cam behind. I swore I would never leave him and that I'd always take care of him. It was an unspoken promise we made to each other. But I couldn't do it anymore. How was I supposed to take care of and protect him – or anyone – when I could barely take care of myself? Our promise – that I'd kept for so many years to the best of my ability – dissipated within the dense fog that clogged my mind.

Part of Cam was very angry with me for deserting him. But, around the time I left, he took on a more protective role of our mom. He was still angry with her and hated her drinking, but he became her ally and I became part of the enemy side, for I dared to open the closet to reveal our skeletons.

It was during this time Cam developed a relationship with our mother that I found disturbing on many levels. It seemed desperate, tunnel-visioned and enabling, on both sides. I think Mom was afraid to lose both of us; Cam thought his presence could change things for the better. Mom had reason to be afraid; Cam was wrong.

The frail fibers that held Mom and Pat's marriage together disintegrated and they separated. She became Heather and Ian's primary caregiver, which meant Pat had to fork over child support. There was a twist: she had to claim it as income. This was a twist she suffered for later on.

Mom drank more. She ballooned to nearly twice her normal weight, and her body failed her. She suffered not one, but two near-fatal heart attacks – she actually flat-lined once. I found out about the heart attacks through the 7-11 clerk she spoke to every day when she went in for her "ciggies and Diet Pepsi." That made my position in my family quite clear.

Mom nearly died. And she was on heart, cholesterol and blood pressure medicines. You'd think that would be enough to convince her to change her lifestyle. Not my mom. In fact, she joked about it. It amazed me how many times she cheated death. Why did God keep sending her back when she obviously wanted to leave so badly?

I never understood.

Chapter Fourteen

The Return To Oz

I know God will not give me any-
thing I can't handle. I just wish that
He didn't trust me so much.
~ Mother Teresa (1910-1997)

Oz is the nickname I often used to refer to
Winnipeg. Not because it was a beautiful, mys-
tical place, but more because a big ass tornado
waited for me there – swirling all the crap I left
behind in its bottomless eye. I finally realized
that problems, heartaches, and painful memories follow us, even when we don't acknowledge
them. They cling like leeches, sucking the life
source out of us. I needed to pour salt all over
myself so everything would shrivel up and die.

I did go back to Winnipeg for a while. I had to
face the demons I left back there, because until
I did, I wasn't living. I'd remain that chick who
sat alone choking down a donated Christmas

dinner. I'd fallen into that hole and needed to figure a way out. To survive, I needed to do three things: re-build relationships with my family (with boundaries in place), accept my grandparents' deaths, and learn to live my life guilt-free.

This was easier said than done.

After a lot of thinking, I called my mom, asking if I could come back home. Heather and Ian were now fifteen and fourteen. The smarter thing to do, of course, would have been to stay with Uncle Craig and go to Mom's for short visits. But I thought that if we all stayed together, somehow, we'd be able to figure things out – or I could.

Leaving Edmonton had been really hard. I had to admit defeat – to myself and to Dad. And even more difficult than that was having to say goodbye to my dad and Robin. He had paid for my way out of the hell I was in and gave me a chance to get back on my feet. He welcomed me into his home and tried enveloping me into his new family. And all I gave him in return was pain, worry, stress and a whole pile of shit. I was so ashamed.

Because I didn't have a phone, I couldn't even call him to say "Goodbye," or "Thanks for trying," or "Sorry." But Robin had a sort of sixth sense about things. When my phone was cut off a few months earlier, she came by once a week to check in on me, bringing me a few cans of things or bags of pasta. I'm not sure she ever told my dad. The day before I left for Winnipeg, she paid me a visit and brought my dad.

Without a phone, they couldn't buzz in, so I had no idea they were at the main door. The door was unlocked, as I was expecting the land-lady to bring papers. Out of the kindness of her heart, she had offered to file an eviction so the break from my lease would be clean – nothing owed. I was in the bedroom taping up the last small box of my possessions when I heard, "Hello?" from the front door.

A cold slush spread from my gut out to my extremities when I recognized Robin's voice. When I turned around and saw Dad with her, I swallowed a huge lump in my throat. I'm not sure Dad knew how bad things had gotten. I didn't know whether Robin told him I had to sell off my stuff, or that Welfare cut me off, or how much trouble I was having finding a job. But he knew then. I walked slowly out of the bedroom, hugging myself.

Dad took in a deep breath through his nose, then slowly blew it back out, shoving his hands into his jeans pockets. Robin, tearing up, rushed over to me and hugged me hard. "Oh Tam..." she said, sniffing.

"So, things are pretty bad, huh?" Dad said, looking around my empty apartment. "I wish you'd told us."

"I did," I said over Robin's shoulder.

Dad shook his head. "No, you didn't. You asked me for money. I can't just hand money over to you. But if you'd told me about Welfare and...this..."

Robin finally let go and moved beside me.

"There's nothing you could have done," I said. "This is my fault. All of it. I'm a big girl now. I should have gotten help when I started falling off the wagon. It's too late now. I have to leave and get some help so I can finally get my shit together."

"What? You're going back to Winnipeg?" Dad said. "Do you really think that's a good idea?"

I smiled, remembering that I was asked the same question before going to Edmonton. "Probably not. But the things I need to deal with are there. And it doesn't seem to matter where I am, that crap follows me. I'm not going to make it anywhere *ever* unless I go back and get help."

"How are you getting back?" he asked.

"Mom is renting a car and driving up with Cam."

Dad rolled his eyes. "So, you're going to fit these things in a car?"

There wasn't much left, really. I sold everything that could be sold. But I had a computer, my clothes, a few stuffed animals and trinkets I got from Grandma.

"I dunno," I said, shrugging. "Whatever fits, fits. Whatever doesn't I'll just leave here."

Then the most unexpected thing happened: Dad walked over and hugged me. He'd hugged me before, but always sort of a walk-by squeeze. That time, he pulled me into his chest, rubbing my arm with his hand. When he spoke, his chest vibrated, his voice cracked: "I wish we could have done more for you. I feel badly that you suffered. But 'helping' isn't 'supporting.' You need to find that strength you had when you first got here – that kept you going. Then you'll be okay."

Then he pulled away, wiping his eyes. Robin gave me one more hug. She paused at the door. "Take care. Keep in touch with us, okay? And if you need us, we're here."

Dad waved. "Once you straighten up, I know you'll be something great. Take care. We love you. Let us know if we can do anything down the road."

The door closing echoed around the apartment. That night I slept on the floor. It wasn't too bad – I still had my comforter and pillow. I stared out the uncovered windows. The sky was clear and black so the stars were bright. It was early spring and still a little chilly, especially since the heat was cut off.

"God," I whispered. "I don't know if what I'm doing is the right decision, but things sure didn't work out very well here. I know I blamed you a lot the last while. I'm sorry. I guess things can't get worse than this, can they? And if this is my 'rock bottom' I guess I need to thank you for helping me survive it. Now I need to ask you to guide me through the next part. And tell Grandma and Grandpa I'll try to see them soon. Thanks. Amen."

The next morning, my mom and Cam showed up. I crammed what I could into the four-door sedan and left the rest in the apartment with a note telling the landlady to take what she wanted for herself and give the rest to any tenants who might need stuff. I locked the door, pulled it shut then shoved the keys back under the door.

Done.

I just hoped what my dad said about my strength was right.

Cam was going to University at that point. He rented a house with three other guys a few streets over, but was always at Mom's for meals. Mom, Ian and Heather lived in a two-bedroom apartment on the upper level of a duplex a few streets over from our old house on Niagara. It wasn't bad but, as always, Mom had way too much stuff. It resembled a well-organized pawnshop. The kids had the bedrooms, while she slept on the couch in the living room. At first, things seemed okay, but then it was worse than living at Dad's, in some ways, because the kids weren't kids anymore – they were both teenagers – and both had been badly affected by what had happened while I'd been sorting (and re-sorting) my own life the past two years.

Neither Heather nor Ian went to school and my mom didn't force them to go. "It's not worth the fight," she said. "They're too big and too strong for me to force them, and I'm too tired to try."

Heather, who was fifteen by then, was on anti-depressants because her depression got so bad she wouldn't get out of bed. And Ian was angry all the time – at everyone. Once, shortly after I arrived, he and my mom had a huge fight. Afterwards, Mom ran off to her bell practice (she was in a bell choir through our church) and

Ian shut himself in his bedroom. A few minutes later, I heard screaming and things crashing. When I opened Ian's door, he was sitting on the floor beside his bed, panting. His bed had been ripped apart and upturned, and he was crying. The room was covered in paper, broken glasses, and ripped up books.

I have no idea what happened to those kids while I'd been missing in action, but they were both in so much pain – just like Cam and I had been so many years before, yet nobody talked about anything.

Once, Ian gave me his opinion of Mom's drinking. Mom was out and Cam, Ian and I were chatting in the living room. We were talking about hilarious memories – the laughter was so nice. Then the mood went serious when Cam noticed the time.

"Shouldn't Mom be back by now?" he said.

Ian blew a raspberry. "Uh, yeah, but it's Dad's payday," he said, sinking back into the loveseat. "She's probably cashing Dad's support check and hitting the liquor store."

I frowned. "What do you mean? What's he paying her for?"

"Child support," Cam said. "Didn't she tell you? Pat gives her half of every paycheck. Gives her the money every two weeks."

"That means she's getting more money than I could earn! Does she give any to you and Heather?"

"Are you crazy?" Ian said. "She has more important things to spend the money on. I mean, what kind of mother takes money her ex gives her to raise her kids and spends it on booze and smokes? Do you know how much money she would have if she didn't do that shit?"

He was right.

I'll give her credit. She did buy groceries and other basics for the kids before she bought anything else – just like when we were kids. But somehow she got herself in so much debt in between paydays. I could not understand how a person with income more than $2500 a month ended up behind in her bills, rent and other debts. Mom always lived way beyond her means. She liked nice things and gave the illusion of "well-off" by displaying those nice things. The normal observer didn't know she hadn't paid for any of them yet. I was more worried about the drugs, though.

I think I was more amazed that someone who had as many health scares as she did, still drank – not to mention reactions with her medications. The woman was on drugs for her heart, asthma, depression and anxiety. Not only that, she also had various pain medications, antihistamines, and other things I didn't recognize. Each bottle had a different doctor's name on it. *What the hell is wrong with doctors, anyway?* I thought. *Shouldn't there be some sort of inquiry into the kinds of medications a person is on before you rip off another prescription? Stupid doctors.*

Within a month, I slipped right back into the role of mother to her children. In compliance with the Separation Agreement, Ian and Heather went to Pat's every two weeks. Apparently, it wasn't any better over there. Pat started drinking heavily, too, and often kept the kids up ranting about my mom. So, the kids never got a break from the chaos. Heather came home from Pat's completely depressed and drained, while Ian came back twice as pissed off as before he'd gone. In a way, it was worse than when Cam and I were kids, because those kids had *no one*. We at least had Uncle Craig and our grandparents. They had two messed up, drunken parents and each other.

To add to the fire, my mom constantly talked about dying and what she wanted done if she died. She wanted me and Cam to take care of Heather and Ian (if she died before they turned eighteen). Then she kept asking me what I wanted from her belongings and told me she wanted me to have her piano and music because I'd "make the best use of it." I finally understood why Uncle Craig and Dorothy wouldn't take Cam and me when we were kids: it gave her an excuse to let go. I didn't like how she was acting, and it scared me that she was talking about death so much, but if I'd agreed to all her requests or signed on to take the kids, I was afraid she'd finally kill herself. I couldn't let her do that to me, Cam or her other kids.

And I wasn't going to let her do that to herself.

On my 29th birthday, after she celebrated with many cocktails, we finally had a blowout that had been brewing since I'd first arrived. Mom drank almost three-quarters a bottle of rum and was still pouring. I poured the rest of my first drink down the kitchen sink.

"What's your problem?" she asked, coughing. She grabbed her inhaler and puffed deeply, then lit up a smoke.

I shook my head and laughed. "Oh my God. Do you realize you could kill yourself using your inhaler while you're drunk *and* smoking?"

She took a long drag that sucked in her cheeks. Then she blew the smoke in my face. "Whatever. Are you my mother now?"

"You know, Cam told me you'd changed," I said. "That's the only reason I agreed to stay here. But I'm cooking for your kids, trying to get them to go to school..."

"Yeah, thanks for all of that by the way," she said, raising her glass to me. "And Happy Fuckin' Birthday." She laughed like a four-pack-a-day smoker, then chugged down the last of her shot.

Rage rose up from the pit of my stomach and stuck in my throat. "Why do you hate me so much?"

She slammed her glass on the coffee table, pulled herself off the couch, and sauntered over to me. She rested her wrist on my shoulder, her cigarette dangling from her fingertips. "I don't hate you," she said, her face inches from mine. "You're my baby girl. I just wish you weren't so...so..."

I turned my head to avoid her skunky breath. "...so much like you?" I asked. "Or so much like you *wanted* to be?"

Mom tried maneuvering her cigarette to her lips, nearly missing. After a long drag, she blew smoke in my face again. "You're so fucking beautiful. And talented. And skinny. And people like you without your half trying. I try, you know. I always tried. Tried with Grandma and Grandpa. Tried with your dad. Tried with you and Cam. Nothing was ever good enough. But you – you were always good enough, weren't ya?"

That was the most honest answer she'd ever given me. Even if it was marinated in alcohol and she didn't remember saying it later on, it was honest. She loved me, but she resented me.

"So what do you want me to do, then?"

She stared at me. Her head wobbled. "Help me die."

I pushed her arm off my shoulder and she stumbled. "I think I should move into my own place. I just can't do this anymore."

The next month, I got a job as Legal Assistant in a wonderful law firm and moved into a two-bedroom apartment. I had no furniture, I slept on an air mattress in the master bedroom and I spent my entire first paycheck on groceries and starter stuff, but it was home – my home. And Mom wasn't allowed to come over or call unless she was sober.

I didn't hear from her often.

After that, many happy things came my way. I made many friends at my job, and my co-workers were like a family. They taught me that it was okay to reach out to others when I was in need. Once, when I needed a little extra money to get me through to the next payday, I asked the office manager, Anita, if I could have an advance on my paycheck.

"If we give you an advance, you know that your next pay will be smaller," she said in a motherly tone. "What if you don't have enough from your next pay to get by? We just don't want you to get yourself into a nasty cycle."

I sat in the cushy chair on the other side of Anita's desk. My stomach growled. I ran out of money to buy groceries and hadn't brought lunch in for a couple of days so I'd have enough for dinners. "I know," I said, staring at the floor. "But I could work overtime or something."

"You already work so hard," she said. "You work through your lunches, you cover the other assistants and you stay later for Barb. Why don't you go back to work and I'll see what I can do, okay? I'll talk to the partners and let you know."

I went back to my desk convinced that I'd have to sneak food from the office fridge or something. Then Anita came back to my desk when all the other assistants went for lunch. She handed me an envelope. "Here," she whispered. "This is a gift from the partners."

She squeezed my shoulder and went around the corner. I opened the envelope and took out a check in the amount of one half of my full pay. I cried. That was how they were with me. So generous, so kind and always encouraging me to be the best I could be. The partner I bonded with the closest, David, reminded me of my grandfather and Mr. Bassey wrapped up into one. He constantly asked about how I was doing, if I was eating enough, if I needed anything. He never let one day go by without saying, "You are a special girl, you know that? *So* special. Don't ever let anyone make you feel less than that." From that job, I got so many things I'd either lost or forgotten about: respect, confidence, self-esteem, self-worth and belief in myself.

Even Auntie Lois, with whom I had weekly lunch dates while I worked there, noticed a difference in me. "You seem happier, my Dear. You have color in your face and it looks...fuller. I'm so proud of you. So, uhm, how is your eating?"

"Good," I said. And it was the truth. I'd gone from making myself throw up anywhere from four to eight times a day to once a week or not at all. "It's all a matter of learning how to deal with stuff, you know?"

She nodded. "Yes. I never thought you did that to lose weight. I think you needed some form of control. That was yours. I'm happy to hear things are better."

God must have felt I was finally ready for another form of love, because around the same time I met my future partner in life, Steve. I knew Steve from when we were teenagers because he was a drinking friend of Cam's. But he was a year younger than Cam, making him three years younger than me, so the timing wasn't right. Then one day when we were picking Cam up at his house, Steve came over to our car to chat until Cam was ready. I didn't even recognize him.

As we drove off, I asked Cam who he was. "It's Steve! Don't you remember him?"

"Yeah," I said. "But he was a scrawny, long-haired skater who drank more than any grown man I knew. Now he's tall, muscular and...well... *hot.*"

"I'll tell him that," Cam said. And the rest is history. Cam and his friends set us up, and we started dating. Being someone who always avoided close relationships, it was so weird to me to feel such a close bond with someone so quickly. It was like I knew when I met him that he was "the one." After a few months of dating, he moved into my apartment. I also started going to University to get my degree in psychology. And, for the first time in several years, I had no debt – and money in the bank. I was strong – physically, mentally and spiritually.

With all the wonderful things going on in my life, I decided it was time to face the one thing I'd tried so hard to push down: my grandparents' deaths. That didn't mean I was ready to accept their death. What it did mean was that I was ready to deal with the feelings I had about it.

It took three tries before I could get near where they rested – Steve went with me each time. The first time, I only made it to the gates and had to leave. The second time, we went into the Information Booth at the front of the cemetery to get a map to where my grandparents' graves were. Once I got the map, I made Steve take me home. Finally, a couple of weeks after that second attempt, I'd taken a couple of days off around my 30th birthday and decided visiting my grandparents was one of the things I was *going* to do. We stopped off at the flower shop so I could buy a purple lily and a holder to put into the ground. Steve drove me right up to their area in the graveyard. I clutched the wrapped flowers in my fist as Steve went around the truck to help me out. We tiptoed through the luscious spongy green grass, hand-in-hand, apologizing to my grandparents' eternal neighbors as we tromped across them. To me there's something eerie and disrespectful about marching across people's graves.

We crept on until we came to a massive headstone right in the middle of a short, crooked row. A golf-ball-sized lump lodged in my throat. I wanted to run but my feet rooted and stood their ground. Steve gripped my shoulder – with an odd but comforting familiarity of Grandpa's hands – and kissed the top of my head. Then, without a word, he slipped back to the truck so I could be alone with my grandparents.

The headstone was larger than I thought it would be – about two feet high and two-and-a-half wide. The outside of the stone was gray, with shiny flecks that sparkled in the sun, similar to the large boulders at the lake. The middle of the stone was polished black, shiny like marble, with their name etched across in thick, bold letters: BATTY. At the base were two nameplates where my grandparents' full names were delicately engraved: George Wilfred Batty and Lillian Mae Worth.

Someone – probably Uncle Craig or Dorothy – planted pansies between their nameplates. A light breeze swept through, tickling the branches of the sturdy elm tree behind me as it danced in time with the pansies. I knelt down to be at eye-level with the headstone. Then I traced all the beautifully crafted letters with my fingertips.

I spoke in a squeaky whisper. "I'm sorry it took me so long to come. I'm sure you've been kept updated about what's been going on. And even if Uncle Craig didn't tell you everything, I'm sure Grandma sent Grandpa out to make sure."

I laughed weakly. When my fingers ran out of letters, I fidgeted with the grass under my knees. The golf ball swelled into a tennis ball.

"I was so angry with both of you for leaving me alone. I never got to say goodbye...or to thank you..."

It took every ounce of strength I had not to leave. I *had* to stay. Letting all of the feelings rise up and be felt was the hardest thing I would ever do, and I knew if I could make it through that moment, anything else I did would be okay. That I'd be okay.

"Thank you for giving me my childhood – for being there when I needed you – for letting me be a kid. Thank you...for saving me. Without your presence, I would never have had the strength to come this far."

Warm streams trickled down my cheeks and the breeze gently tossed my hair back over my shoulders, like Grandma used to do when she wanted to see my face.

"I can't promise you I'll never mess up again. But just like Grandma said, I'll 'take what I need and let the rest go.' I'll never derail again. At least I'll try not to."

I shoved a plastic flower holder in the middle of the dancing pansies and put the oversized, purple lily inside it.

"I won't be back for a long time, but I know now what Grandpa meant in the hospital – you'll always be with me."

I touched my head, my heart and then the headstone – the same way Grandpa said goodbye to me. As I made my way back to the truck, images of my childhood passed through my mind: the five-year old girl listening in on phone calls; Grandma's bear hugs; afternoon teas; canoe rides with Grandpa; my confirmation; and their funerals. Oddly, by the time I got to the truck, I was full.

The aching emptiness I'd clung to for so long was filled with contentment, love and happiness. Steve started up the truck and grabbed my hand. How lucky I was. I wished Grandpa and Grandma could have met Steve.

I looked back one last time at the headstone and was surprised to see two glorious bluebirds perched on top of it – Grandpa's favorite bird. Bluebirds are rare in that area. They stared at me and I didn't think it at all strange that they watched us drive away. They turned around as the truck drove off. Pebbles spat out from under the truck's wheels. When we'd driven around the corner out of sight, I saw two blue streaks shoot up over the trees, circle, then fly off.

I smiled.

A few months after my visit, a couple of weeks before Christmas 2001, Steve got a job offer in Edmonton and I went with him. As we drove out of the city limits, all our belongings in the trailer behind us, I was relieved.

This time, my departure felt good.

I had no regrets, no fears, and all my demons were put to rest. The door of my past shut behind me with only a tiny peephole to glimpse through when I wanted to reminisce. I knew I'd never go back to Winnipeg, but it didn't matter. I had what was most important to me and a new life ahead of me. Steve and I had much happiness ahead of us. But even as I watched the city get smaller in the rearview mirror – I knew there'd still be things to face from a distance.

PART IV:

FULL CIRCLE

Chapter Fifteen

From A Distance

Accept the things to which fate
binds you, and love the people with
whom fate brings you together, but
do so with all your heart.
~ Marcus Aurelius (121-180)

Edmonton the second time around was much
sweeter. It's not to say I didn't have hard times
but I wasn't alone anymore. I was also a different person.

In my early twenties, I changed my last
name from Nicol back to Laird. When I did so, I
added two names to my identification: Arlene,
which was my mom's birth name, and Chynna,
which was one of the unique names my parents
tossed around before I was born. Dad wanted to
give me a hippie name; my mom wanted
different, but not so different I'd be defending it
every recess. Even though Chynna was techni-

cally my first name, I only started using it after I moved back to Edmonton with Steve. It seemed appropriate: new life, new name. Tami was put to rest so Chynna could be born.

The most significant thing that happened during that time was that I got pregnant. Secretly, Steve and I had been trying for over three years to conceive with no luck. I knew it would be difficult due to my past issues with infections to my reproductive organs and a battle with cervical cancer.

Then, once I did get pregnant, I was told I probably wouldn't be able to carry the baby to term because I had a bicornuate uterus. My doctor discovered that lovely piece of information at my first ultrasound at seven weeks. The early ultrasound was a precaution because of my history. When the technician didn't tell me anything and wouldn't show me whether there was a heartbeat or anything, I knew something was up.

"I'll be right back, Ms. Laird," the tech said, patting my hand. "I need to get the attending doctor."

I didn't say anything. She left me alone in the dimmed room with Seventies tunes on the speakers. I rolled my eyes and squeezed them shut, warm trickles sliding down my cheeks into my hair. Steve couldn't come with me because he couldn't get the time off work, so I had to face the fact alone. *It was happening again,* I thought. *Another miscarriage.*

Oh well. We'll try again.

Just when I wondered how bad it would have been to release my too full bladder, the doctor came into the room. After quick introductions, he picked up the ultrasound wand and pressed the same spots on my lower abdomen. Both of them stared at the monitor I wasn't permitted to see. Then the doctor tossed the wand onto the side table, shoved his glasses up onto the top of his head and leaned back in the rolling chair. He folded his hands over his swollen belly and said, "You are scared, no?"

What, was he kidding? Having me drink water until my bladder was about to explode, then having two people press on it for the past hour wasn't torturous enough? My heart pounded, my mouth was dry and I chewed the inside of my bottom lip – partially to stop tears and partially because I was so nervous, it was getting difficult to stop my overfull bladder from exploding.

"Baby seems fine, my Dear," he said. "The problem is that your uterus dips down here, you see?" He shoved the screen around so I could watch while he pointed. "This is called a bicornuate. Many women give birth to healthy babies who have this condition. Our main concern for you right now is that your baby has attached itself very close to the fallopian tube opening. These next few weeks we need to watch closely and see which side of the opening baby develops on. We'll get you to come back in two weeks. Try not to worry."

I would hear this way too many times during that pregnancy.

Steve and I had planned to go away to Jasper that weekend. We decided that whatever was going to happen would happen whether or not we went away. What happened was that Steve proposed to me that weekend. It was perfect. He took me to a beautiful area by the Athabasca River. Somehow I knew in the moment I said, "Yes!" that we'd be okay. And so would our baby. But I was still scared.

Not only was I late starting a family at thirty-two, I wondered how I could even think of getting pregnant when I had no clue how to be a mother. What if I didn't have any maternal instincts? What if I abused the baby the way I was abused? What if I gave the baby every reason to hate me and never speak to me again? What if I was like my mother?

Once we got past the first trimester and found out baby was growing on the "right" side of the fallopian tube opening, we told two family members: Uncle Craig and his wife Dorothy. I swore them to secrecy, which killed him, because he was so excited. But he understood. "That's all you need is to have your mom calling you every night in a drunken stupor. With your history you need to be calm. Mum's the word."

After that, I worried, stressed, panicked, and cried to the end of the nine long months – partly because I was a high-risk pregnancy, and I wanted my baby to be healthy, but more because I was scared that if my mom found out about the baby, she'd force herself into my life again. There was no way I could let her come near my child after everything she did to me and let happen to me. Plus, I'd heard disturbing things from home that only intensified my fears.

I didn't have much contact with my mom, but I did communicate with my siblings through email and phone calls. Bearing in mind every story had two sides, I took everything I heard with a grain of salt. If the source was a trusted one – like Uncle Craig or Dorothy – it held more water.

Then one event pretty much nailed the coffin lid shut in terms of my feelings about Mom being around my child. It was Cam who called me. His voice shook and I knew something bad happened between him and Mom.

"I wanted you to hear this from me," he said.

Mom, Heather, Ian and Cam moved into a five-bedroom townhouse in the same complex we'd lived in when Cam and I were kids. I wondered whether they still had 'hood parties.

I had no idea why Cam had chosen to put himself in that position but, as Dorothy and Auntie Lois kept reminding me, "Campbell is a grown man. You can't save him anymore. You need to concentrate on you and your baby. Campbell will do what he's going to do."

I still worried.

"What happened?" I asked.

Cam released a heavy sigh. "Mom's in the psych ward."

Okay. That got my attention.

He told me in great detail how he and Mom had seen an advertisement for a call for extras in a production to be filmed in Winnipeg. Excited about the prospects of getting discovered, they splurged on some celebratory cocktail mixtures – rum and Diet Pepsi – and worked on their talent resumes together.

He said things were great at first. They'd had a good time – had a few drinks then practiced their singing and stuff.

Then all hell broke loose. My mom was quite fun with a few drinks in her, but when she went just one sip over her limit, things grew overcast. She became angry, spiteful and picked fights.

He didn't go into great detail about what caused the fight, but she was famous for pushing buttons she knew would trigger people to retaliate. I guessed that's what had happened because Cam said she'd pushed him and pushed him and got in his face. He'd told her he'd had enough, then turned his back to her. As he walked away, my mom grabbed a butter knife off the kitchen counter and plunged it into his back.

In all of my life, she slapped me, punched me, choked me, called me names a truck driver wouldn't use, threw me down the stairs, threw me out of the house and even threw knives *at* me. But never did she do anything like that. My silence prompted him to continue.

"Thank God the kids were at Pat's," he said.

Yes, thank God.

"I called the cops and with a knife wound, I had to hold her down until they got there. They took her to the psych ward to sober up. They're supposed to give her a psychological evaluation to determine whether she can be released. They also asked me if I wanted to press charges."

"And you are, right?" I asked.

Cam didn't answer.

"Cam, you *have* to press charges. It's the only way to get her help. C'mon, Cam. This is the first time Mom has gone past the point of no return. People will finally understand what we've been saying all these years."

Cam clicked his tongue. "I just can't think about it right now, Tam."

It must have been so hard for him. What happened probably didn't even sink in yet. His own mother tried to kill him.

But it was our last chance. "Cam, if it had been me..."

"...Mom would be in jail right now, I know. I'm not you. She and I don't have the history you do. I just can't think about it. Not right now."

He was going to just let it go. I knew it.

"Cam, if you wait too long, she'll be released. You know damn well she's smart enough to say what she needs to. She'll fool them into thinking it was all because she drank too much."

"Pat went to see what's going on. I'll call you back," he said.

"Cam?"

"What?"

"Are you okay?"

"Yeah."

"For real? You aren't just saying that to shut me up, right? You're...okay?"

"Tam, it wasn't bad enough for me to go to the hospital or anything. I'm fine. For real. Call you later. Take care of *you*, okay? You and the baby."

Just like I predicted, my mom fooled the evaluator into thinking she was sane and she was released. Once again, she escaped responsibility for something horrible she did, and not one person around her did a thing about it. They didn't even talk about it. But after that, Cam was scared of her. He never drank with her again. He fell into the same state of mind I had been in after Grandpa died. He couldn't hold down a job, he became depressed, and suffered from nightmares about what happened to him.

What kind of God allows things like that to happen – over and over and over again? I thought. *Just give her what she wants, damn it! C'mon! What has to happen before you just take her already? How much do we, or she, have to suffer?*

The experience proved what I feared the most: the longer Mom was left untreated, the worse she became. How sad that even at the point when the White Elephant could be seen – by everyone – people still refused to deal with it. Our mother wasn't just irresponsible and threatening, she was dangerous. And I was about to make this woman a grandmother.

Sweet.

I worried and stressed so much after that phone call that I began having severe Braxton Hicks cramps. I knew I had to rest and avoid any unnecessary stress for the rest of my pregnancy.

There was no way I was going to let my mom's lifestyle steal my baby too.

Thankfully, Jaimie, my first child, was born January 26, 2003. With her porcelain skin and ocean blue eyes, she resembled one of those china dolls from the early 1900s.

My fears intensified. It was different when Jaimie was inside of me. Inside, I could protect her. Outside of me she was vulnerable. Ever since the stabbing incident I was terrified of what my mom was capable of, and most of all, how she reacted to things. Uncle Craig was scared she would drive up to Edmonton and force herself on us or take legal action to have access to Jaimie. Even my Uncle Rick, who did his best to stay away from Mom and her antics, called me and said, "I won't tell your Mom about Jaimie. You tell her when you're ready – not because you feel guilty or you're afraid of her."

I did tell my dad, though. He was proud and excited. I think part of him was hurt I didn't tell him I was pregnant; but, without having to discuss reasons in too much detail, he understood. Somehow, word about what my mom did to Cam made its way to Dad, too.

Six months went by. The guilt was too overwhelming for me. I decided to tell my mom about her grandchild. Maybe, I thought, it would be the one thing to save her. For hours I practiced what to say to her. I had to be strong and not succumb to any manipulation. While Steve had a nap with Jaimie, I dialed Mom's number. My hands were icy cold and shaky. My heart pounded in my ears. Why, at my age, did I still let her make me feel that way? I chatted with Heather and Ian first. Then Ian got Mom.

We carried on with small talk for a few minutes – something I just hated. I always considered small talk to be verbal diarrhea. I think she suspected something. Her voice was cautious. Calm.

I told her about Jaimie – what she looked like, her birth weight, her quirks, my pregnancy and the birth. For a brief moment, I had a taste of what other moms and daughters were like. There's nothing like the mutual experience of pregnancy and birth to bring women together. Then reality checked back in: "So, when can I come meet her?" She didn't even seem offended that I hadn't told her about Jaimie.

I closed my eyes. "I know about what happened with Cam a few months ago, Mom. He told me."

Silence. "Now, look Tam. I don't know what Cam told you, but..."

"He told me everything."

"I want to tell you what really happened..."

"Mom, just because I haven't been there for a while doesn't mean I don't know how things work. I've been there. It's not the first time you guys have fought when you drink. It's just the first time things went as far as they did."

I didn't come right out and say, "It's the first time you stabbed anyone." Even I avoided coming right out with it. But I also knew that one has to be careful in how things are discussed. Especially now that I had a child to think about.

Static echoed in the phone. The fridge kicked back in. Kids playing out in the courtyard outside happily squealed. "I'll let you come up here under one condition: you can't drink."

"Tam, I don't..."

I interrupted. "And I don't just mean no drinking while you're here. If I hear about any more situations like this last one, if I hear about you harassing Cam, if anyone tells me you call or visit them when you're drunk, or I even suspect you've been drinking during your visit, you'll never be allowed to come here again. Got it?"

"I understand." Mom would have said anything at that point to be allowed to come see her granddaughter. For the few weeks before her visit, she was good. Cam said she was excited and "high." She bragged about Jaimie to anyone who would listen, told them she was visiting soon, and showed pictures.

Great, just what I wanted to hear. She was crazy excited and "up." This was not a good sign.

The visit started off okay. Mom came up with Heather. They came over right after they'd checked into their hotel and it was wonderful. They didn't force themselves on Jaimie, but my mom did try holding her. She had tears in her eyes as she reached out to my child. "Please. I just have to hold her. She looks just like her pictures."

Reluctantly, I handed Jaimie to her.

"Oh my God, you are so beautiful," she said, crying. "You look just like your Mama, sweet wee Jaimie."

A wave of warmth washed over me as Mom cooed and cuddled Jaimie. Was that how she was with me? Did she ever hold me that way? When you watched my mom with children – especially babies – the goodness in her shone through, even if just for a moment. Unfortunately, Jaimie screamed until Mom gave her back to me.

There was no pressure, no talk of the past, no pretending. Mom and Heather just enjoyed interacting with Jaimie. But my mother seemed uncomfortable, and she couldn't make eye contact with me. I wondered whether it was because she was jealous that my life turned out the way she wanted hers to, or if she knew – for one reason or another – that she and Jaimie would never have what I had with my grandparents.

The next day my mom showed up alone because Heather "wasn't feeling well." I got close enough to her to tell that she was hung over. She still reeked like booze. I chewed on the inside of my cheek, trying to bring down my rapid heartbeat.

She stayed for a few hours then left.

I don't know why I was disappointed or surprised. She was excited before she left and it was only a matter of time before she drank. I just hoped she could have waited until after her visit. It explains why Heather didn't come with her on the last day. She was probably up all night long, waiting for Mom to come home from... wherever. The hotel bar? A local one?

Jaimie screamed every time Mom came close to her. Some say babies have a sixth sense about people. Jaimie did, and I listened.

I never allowed Mom to come visit again.

In the summer of 2004, Cam called me. He was ecstatic.

"I'm engaged!"

He met a beautiful girl named Tiffany. I was a bit concerned they'd rushed into things as they'd only met a couple of months before. But I knew Cam would never give his heart to just anyone. I also knew Tiffany was strong or he never would have invited her to be a part of our insanity.

My mom, of course, hated her. Or at least that's what she told me. I told Cam not to worry, because she didn't like Steve either. Our partners in life made us strong. They were supportive, loving and protective. I can tell you if my mom *had* shown up and demanded to see Jaimie after I told her not to, she wouldn't have made it in the door. Steve doesn't tolerate crap – especially if it hurts his family. Tiffany was the same.

Mom didn't like not being part of every aspect of our lives. She blamed Steve for being banned from my home and, therefore, refused to let Tiffany take Cam away.

Oddly Cam and Tiffany let my mom plan and carry out their entire wedding. When I asked Cam what he was thinking, he said, "She owes me. And if I don't let her help, she'll ruin it somehow."

He had a good point.

So, with the help of many, and without me – I'd just had our second child, Jordhan – Cam and Tiffany were married that winter. I was so proud of them. The only advice I gave to Cam was,

"You deserve happiness and your wife deserves to enjoy a life with you and without Mom to steer it. Get away. Far away."

That's exactly what he did. He and Tiffany went to teach English in South Korea. He bought his time for a few months, kept the waters calm, then left.

After that, my mom had no Cam. And no Tam. Even with the two children she had still at home, she was lost.

In the spring of 2005 I received more emails from my mom than I had the entire time since we reconnected. I was concerned because her emails spilled over with excitement or sorrow one day, anger the next, then I didn't hear from her for weeks or months. Granted, she kept herself busy: she managed to continue her bell-ringing performances, she still taught piano. She told me she was bored of teaching because she didn't have students that excited her. She was always looking for the next Mozart or Beethoven.

But her behavior and health became more erratic. She spent many hours online chatting in Scottish chatrooms. She made several friends – men, mostly. Cam and I joked that she was looking for a rich man to take her away to some exotic Scottish castle and take care of her for the rest of her life.

She wrote me to say she invited some Scottish guy she'd only talked to online to Winnipeg to stay with her. Not only that, but she was going to travel across Canada with him. She seemed to have reverted back to the impulsive behavior that ruled her when Cam and I were kids.

In the fall of 2005, Mom wrote me often, and a bit too casually, about how she was in and out of the emergency room for her blood pressure and breathing problems. At one point, she wrote,

"My bp was, like, 220/180 or something like that. I couldn't breathe. The ER people had me hooked up to a heart monitor, a blood pressure machine and oxygen. They told me if I didn't stop smoking, and change my lifestyle, I'd die. They even told me I was lucky to be alive. LOL! What do they know? I'll be around until I'm 150."

I knew that normal blood pressure is about 120/80. Of course it depends on the person's size, health history and lifestyle, but 220/180 is one foot in the grave.

Did she stop smoking? Stop drinking? Start exercising? Eat healthier? Take her medication properly?

No.

It should have been a sign. But she didn't see.

Chapter Sixteen

Time's Up

Even the darkest soul passes, at
least once in life, a ray of awareness
of the supernatural, sometimes at
the birth of a child or the death of
a soul.
~ Dagobert D. Runes (1902–1982)

Spring 2006
Emails from my mom became less frequent.
In March, she wrote me an email begging me to
let her come to visit my girls: "As you know, my
grandmother died when I was very young, so I
never got to have a relationship with her. You
were very lucky to have the relationship you had
with Grandma. Oh, Grandma would have just
loved having more little girls around to spoil,
wouldn't she? I can just see her wanting to dress
them up in frilly dresses and take them out to
show them off. Please, Tam. I just want to know

Jaimie. And I want to meet Jordhan. They don't even know me."

I felt horrible and guilty. But I had to stick to my decision. She hadn't slowed down in her party lifestyle. And as long as alcohol was her friend, she couldn't be around my kids. I read her email and left it in my inbox.

I'll write her tomorrow, I thought. *When I'm in a better frame of mind*.

Steve and I talked about having another baby. Neither of us was sure another baby would be a great idea, especially since sleep was a luxury with Jaimie's special needs. But something inside of me told me to try just one more time. I always wanted a little boy to love and spoil. My girls were delicious, but a boy would have completed the picture somehow.

I had a miscarriage in February – just before I heard from Mom. Oddly, I wasn't as devastated by the loss as I thought I'd be. I felt like maybe God wanted us to wait just a little bit longer. Since I was in the middle of a semester at school, and Jaimie was about to be assessed (for the third time) for her "odd" behavior, being pregnant wasn't something I thought I could deal with on top of everything else. But, as fate would have it, a month later, at the end of March, I was pregnant again. This was around the time Mom emailed me.

All of April, I was so sick. I couldn't keep anything down. I had a feeling from the start that a boy grew inside of me; it just felt different. I started having weird dreams. I chalked it up to pregnancy hormones, but the dreams stole much-needed sleep from me. One night in particular, I had a dream that woke me in a cold sweat.

My mom was in it. She was there at the side of my bed, just like when I was little. She did the "...I love you bigger than the whole world..." routine. Her *Timeless* perfume wafted around. She looked happy – *really* happy. Almost relieved.

"What are you doing here?" I asked.

"Xander."

"What?"

"Name him Xander."

"What are you talking about, Mom?"

"Name him Xander. And enjoy them. They don't stay small forever. You miss so much when you pay attention to everything else but them."

"Mom...?"

"I'm going home. Forgive me."

I woke up. My heart pounded. I just made it to the bathroom before my evening snack made a reappearance.

I thought I wouldn't be able to go back to sleep but, oddly, I was content. I collapsed into a comatose-state sleep. The best sleep I'd had in years.

The next evening, Steve, the girls and I were enjoying a lovely dinner when I noticed the phone flash for our attention. We always turned the ringer off during dinnertime. Nothing could be so important it had to interrupt suppertime. While we cleaned up, I listened to the message. It was Uncle Craig.

His voice cracked. "Tam. I know you're probably eating right now, but I need to talk to you. I don't care what time it is, you need to call me. It's very important. If I'm not at home, call me on my cell. Bye."

My heart skipped a beat. I already knew why he called. Steve entertained the girls in the living room while I called Uncle Craig.

He answered on the second ring. "Are you sitting down?"

Oh God. A sitting down call. "I am now," I said. "What's going on?"

"Tam. I have just horrible news for you. Your mom died last night."

Uncle Craig and I made a pact many years earlier that if either of us heard my mom had died, we'd call the other. Because we both had the same non-existent relationship with her, we joked we'd only find out about her death in the newspaper – just like everyone else.

"Was she drunk?" I asked.

"I don't know. Heather found her this morning. I guess your Mom slept too long so Heather went in to see if she was okay and..."

"Oh my God. Poor Heather."

"I know. Your mom's doctor came over and pronounced her dead. The cause of death right now is a heart attack. She didn't even know it was coming, Tam. It was like she went to bed and died. It happened around midnight."

I shivered. That's when I woke up.

Well, that was it, wasn't it? All those years of hate, anger, resentment, blame, secrets – gone. I wasn't sure how to feel. She'd left her White

Elephants behind for the rest of us to deal with. My eyes burned. "I'm really not too sure how to feel about this. I mean, I'm not surprised or shocked. Just not ready, you know?"

Uncle Craig cleared his throat. "I do know..."

I've waited for that phone call all my life. Why *now*? Why at this time in my life, when I am pregnant and happy, did God choose to take her? Why hadn't he taken her years earlier when she *begged* to go?

"Tam, I'll call you tomorrow. Let it sink in a bit and we'll talk some more, okay?"

"I have to go to an assessment for Jaimie tomorrow."

"Concentrate on that. I know it's hard to hear this, but your mom would have wanted you to concentrate on your kids. You know that much, right?"

I hung up the phone. My body was heavy. I lugged myself up the stairs. Jaimie and Jordhan squealed in the bathtub.

Steve met me in the hallway outside of the bathroom.

"Everything okay?"

"My mom died."

"Oh Tam..."

He hugged me. I cried just a little, then bathed my kids.

I'll deal with Mom tomorrow, I thought.

Uncle Craig and Dorothy carried out a lot of the funeral arrangements. They emailed me daily to ask how I felt about this or that. It was just – weird. I still expected Mom to email me or call me, begging to come visit. I waited for drunken phone calls. Nothing came. Uncle Craig and I had many conversations over the weeks before the memorial service. "I loved her," he said. "She was my sister. But it was hard to love her. And I have so much anger left inside I don't know what to do with..."

I understood.

"As hard at this may be to hear, Tam, she did love you guys. It may have been in a desperate obsessive way but she loved you."

That *was* hard to hear. And I wasn't convinced. "The best she could, I suppose."

Isn't it funny, how once a person dies, no matter what a jerk they may have been, people always try to find something nice to say? Why is that? Why not get up in front of God and everyone else and say, "My mom never wanted me, she abused me, she drank herself to death, and we all stood around and did nothing. Yes, let's remember her."

That's what was in my heart. That was the truth, though people phoned and sent cards and emails about what a wonderful person she was and how much she loved us, until I felt like gagging. I knew I couldn't go to her funeral. I waffled for a week about whether to go or not and, in the end, decided it would be best for everyone if I stayed in Edmonton. Besides, my bitterness would have only clouded the ceremony and intensified other people's feelings. Plus, I had to think of my baby. Ironic isn't it? How one life goes and another grows in its place?

Anyone we told about my mom's death had the same reaction I did: stunned but not surprised. She lived on borrowed time. The day of her funeral, I sent a bouquet of flowers: white roses, lilies, and lilies of the valley – all of her favorites. I sent a letter to be read at the service. And I found out the service would be recorded for Cam (who was still teaching in Korea) and me.

I went into my garden during the time others were attending her funeral in Winnipeg. I dug, planted and weeded until my hands were caked with dirt and sweat beaded on my forehead. Dorothy called me when the service was over.

"It went great," she assured me. "Your flowers were gorgeous and we put them up on the memory table."

My letter was read. Uncle Craig told me there wasn't a dry eye in the place.

My mom thought no one would show up at her funeral, but there were as many people at her service as those of my grandparents *combined*. People cared. They loved her. But it is so hard to watch someone kill themselves and not be able to help them. People didn't forget her when they walked away; they simply couldn't stand by and watch her destroy herself.

It was what Uncle Rick said that got to me, though. "That was a beautiful letter you wrote, Tam. Very well written and so articulate. And it said so much without going into detail. The way things have always been. Take care of yourself. *Now* you can."

I had just started writing full-time, juggling many projects and clients on the go, so his words meant so much to me. Uncle Craig told me that he and Uncle Rick had gotten closer in the weeks after Mom's death. Cam was in bliss with his beautiful wife. Heather and Ian both got jobs and seemed happier. It's like a huge cloud of darkness that surrounded all of us cleared away, and we were all finally able to live our lives the way we wanted to – the way we were meant to.

It felt good.

The following week, I received a package with a tape of the funeral, the transcripts, and a copy of the program. I held that tape in my hand for several minutes before putting it up on the media shelf above the TV. I wasn't ready when it first came. I tried to watch it, but when I got to the part where Auntie Lois sang "The Lord Is My Shepherd," I stopped it.

It wasn't for the same reasons I couldn't deal with Grandpa or Grandma's funeral. I had intense anger floating around and I just couldn't sit there and watch people pay tribute to a woman who caused so much distress and pain. Just because she was dead didn't mean I forgot – or forgave.

Once Xander (yes, I named him Xander) was safely outside of me and in my arms, I watched the video. With Steve beside me and Xander nestled in my lap, we rolled the tape.

For the first several minutes of the video, Dorcas, the church pianist/organist, played various hymns while people found seats. The camera panned the congregation, so I saw many faces. Some I suspected would be there. Some I was surprised to see. Auntie Lois, Susan, some of my mom's students, Diane (one of Mom's childhood friends who cut ties with her), some of Pat's family, a few members of her bell choir, the daughter of Muriel (the woman who'd beaten her up), Dorothy's father, summer neighbors from the lake, people she hadn't talked to since I was a child. The list went on. I thought, *Man. Mom must be looking down right now with tears in her eyes.*

"You see, Mom?" I thought, *"People did care. They didn't come just to make sure you were really dead, like you thought they would. They came because they loved you."*

The camera panned to a table set up in the front of the church with a framed picture of my mom surrounded by tiny musical instruments: a handbell, a harp, and piano music. I remembered the picture. Uncle Rick took it the Christmas we got our plane tickets to Orlando. She sat on Grandpa's green barrel chair with her knees tucked up and in her best pose.

As the ceremony started, Pat, Ian, Heather, Uncle Craig, Dorothy, Uncle Rick, his wife Kate and my four cousins all walked in and sat in the first set of pews reserved for family. I rocked with Xander to the minister's voice: "Dear Friends: We are united today by a common sorrow, a common affection, and a common hope. We have come together to give thanks for the life of Janet Nicol, to remember the ways her life touched our own..."

I closed my eyes as the minister prayed and led the congregation into the first hymn. (All the hymns Dorothy chose were the same ones played at Grandpa's funeral. She said, "Your Mom chose the hymns for Grandpa. We figured they meant something special to her so we chose them for her, too.")

The camera panned upward to make me face my enemy: the stained glass window. Oddly, though, it looked different. For my mom's funeral, it was sunny, warm and calm. Christ's eyes shone their beautiful luminescent aquamarine. He was happy.

"...we pause now, and in the silence, let us all give thanks to God for the ways in which Janet's life has touched our own."

In the silence, I stared at Christ. I finally understood. Judas, his back to Christ, guilt etched his face. All the other Disciples faced Him, adored Him, loved Him, yet Jesus reached out to Judas. It was because Judas was the only one who truly needed Him.

As I learned in my Confirmation classes, Christ comes to and reaches out to those who need Him the most. Only He can't help those who turn away until they turn to Him. Mom was Judas, in every sense of the meaning. And now He smiled because Mom finally turned to Him.

I shivered.

Then Auntie Lois sang her solo, "The Lord Is My Shepherd." It was hard to hear her beautiful voice and not be overcome with emotion. I allowed it this time. At the end of her song, I swear Auntie Lois looked up with a small smile as if to say, "Amen, Janet. Amen."

Dorothy asked Auntie Lois how she got through the song with so many memories – good and bad – of our mother. Auntie Lois answered, "It was difficult, but I just pretended Janet and I were singing a duet, just like we did so many years ago. And it made it easier."

Then the most difficult part. The Eulogy. I paused the movie to compose myself. Steve put his strong hand over mine and nodded.

"...and so, I look for the brightest threads that run through the fabric of the life I am celebrating and trust that the background will be visible to the discerning eye."

The minister chose to speak of the good in a person and left the rest for us to bury on our own. And that was how it should be. We could talk about my mom's drinking, her mental illness, her anger but there were good things the bad overshadowed. The time for anger should be gone. At least for now.

The minister talked about Mom's love for music and nature; her love for West Hawk Lake and her students. She even brought up Mom's sense of humor and her contagious belly laugh.

"Many of the life lessons that will remain in her children and grandchildren come from her passion for music."

True.

"Janet was blessed to have friends and companions who accompanied her and sustained her on her journey through life."

Oh man! That had to be the most beautifully crafted understatement I'd ever heard. But Mom *was* blessed. She never hit rock bottom or suffered for too long because friends, family and companions were always there for her.

Then, the words that shot me in the heart: "Most precious to her were her four children. Despite times of challenge and struggle, Janet loved her kids, and they so clearly loved her. That love will be a powerful force for them as they learn to live their lives without her."

My eyes flooded with tears. My chin quivered.

Then, the minister read my letter:

Dear Mom:

I'm sorry I can't physically be here – I know you understand why. There are many things I could say to you, but I really wanted to share what I'm most grateful to you for.

I think what I value most is your appreciation and talent for art and music. All four of your kids have varying degrees of your talents: artwork, singing, playing instruments, and writing. I remember being frustrated and angry at having to get up early to practice piano or go to choir practices; but they are some of my fondest memories and greatest treasures. I don't just "hear" music – I feel it and it touches my soul. I don't just sing a song, I put passion into the music and words so perhaps it can touch others the same way; and I don't just "jot words down on paper," I write in such a way that my readers relate my words to their own experiences.

You gave these gifts to me, Mom, and for that, I am eternally grateful to you. Your talent for and appreciation of the arts and music will live on in us kids. And you have to know, it's also been passed on to your granddaughters – when I see them move and wiggle to music; when I see them singing songs with so much happiness; and when they draw pictures far beyond what they should be able to, I think of you.

Thank you: for deciding to give me life; for loving me even though love was difficult for you; and for trying to the best of your ability. I hope you've finally found peace where you are.

Love, Tam

Tears fell down my cheeks. That letter took me days to write. But it seemed to say it all.

They buried half of my mom's ashes with Grandma and Grandpa. The rest were to be kept for her children to carry out her final wishes. As the tape came to an end, the minister spoke once more:

"We can never replace Janet, who is gone. Yet we can give new hope, love and security to those who mourn her most deeply. When we know that we have that kind of love and support, it is so much easier for us to stand here today and say to God, 'God, here is Janet – our mother, our sister, our beloved friend,' and believe that God has welcomed Janet with open arms into her heavenly home. Amen."

We kept Mom's ashes until Cam came back from Korea in the spring of 2007. Susan's family generously donated their dock (their cabin was still two doors from Grandpa's cabin) so we could carry out Mom's final wish: to be sprinkled over West Hawk Lake. Actually, she also had an idea to be sprinkled at the Titanic site, but we figured it would be easier to carry out the former wish.

The water was calm – like glass. Cam and Ian gently guided a canoe to the middle of the lake. As the paddles sliced into the surface of the water, the quiet magnified each stroke. Once at the perfect spot, they stopped paddling and let the canoe come to a stop where it wanted to.

They sat as the water licked the sides of the boat. Then each of them said a hushed prayer and released Mom's ashes to the one place she'd always found peace: the cool, clear, deep waters of West Hawk Lake.

As her ashes mixed with the lake, I silently hoped the part we'd given to the water had her heart. For her heart was the one part of her that truly belonged there.

> *God of peace, who brings light out of the darkness, new life out of death, we give you thanks for the gift of life, especially for Janet's life.*
>
> *Amen.*

Afterword

And in the end the love you take is
equal to the love you make.
~ The Beatles

"Everything in life happens for a reason –
good and bad," my grandfather used to tell me
often. "You don't learn to appreciate the good
unless there's a struggle or two." I don't think I
fully understood the wisdom in Grandpa's pearls
until recently. And this book was entirely based
on that premise.

This book has been a long time in the making
and I'm proud of the way it turned out. I'm sure
it will be a tough read for many as it was for me
to write. The first draft I wrote the day after my
mom died was filled with anger, blame, and
pain – all the negative emotions I'd had bottled
up inside for so many years that I never got the
chance to resolve with her. That draft was more
of a regurgitation – getting everything out as
fast as possible. Then I let it sit for a few months
until I could go back to it with clearer thoughts
and a more positive purpose. Had I published

that version, the message intended in the book would have been lost. I meant it to help others draw strength from the "bad," use that strength to journey through life and – the hardest for me – to forgive.

Like many people in similar situations, I could have been a statistic. I could have listened to the negative tapes playing in my head. I could have taken to heart the words said to me in anger, believed that I'd never amount to anything. I could have given up. But I refused.

"Give up" has never been in my vocabulary no matter what hurdles I've had to face. My mom gave up, and we gave up on her. And that's why I can't give up nor am I willing that anyone else would. Giving up is the easy way out; it takes courage and strength to go on no matter what life throws your way. I'm not saying that I'm always courageous or strong – I have my moments of self-doubt. But I try...I stay and fight and try...and we all need to do that.

No child should ever have to endure what my brother and I lived through. In some ways, we still re-live many of those experiences today – how could we not? There are times I encounter an experience, or meet someone new, or hear a sound that's oddly familiar, or a smell that reminds me of...something...and I'm taken back. I relive it for a few minutes. But I don't let it stay here in the present. I take what I need from that experience...that one moment...then file it back away where it belongs. We can't let the past stay in the present or we'll never have a future! When I find myself slipping backward into depression or anxiety, I remind myself of that. It's okay to take the memories out occasionally when, say, helping others through a similar situation, or to give me a needed kick in the pants to keep moving forward. It took a very long time before I was finally able to do that, but it's important.

I'm finally in a place where I can embrace all that's happened to me with open arms. My experiences have helped me be a better, stronger, enlightened, deeper individual. I've gained a level of insight into my children's special needs I might not otherwise have had. I pay attention to the small things that go on around me because, sometimes, those small things matter more than the bigger things. I live for today because tomorrow might not happen. I'm not afraid to speak up on important issues. Others may be uncomfortable or afraid to discuss them but someone has to get people talking about them.

I got my degree in Psychology (ironically enough), which has given me tremendous insight into my mom's condition, our family's reaction to it, and better ways of coping. And, most importantly, it's helped me learn to love and be loved without fear.

Grandpa was right: everything in life does happen for a reason. And my mom's life wasn't an accident. Would she have gotten better had we taken the steps to get her help? Would she still be alive if she'd gotten the help she needed? We'll never know. The lack of answers to these questions are what prevent me from giving up on myself. I don't want to leave people behind wondering the same things about me.

My mom was a gift from God and her life had a purpose, the same as the rest of us. It doesn't matter what she did or didn't do anymore. What matters is that those of us she left behind must learn to live our lives to the fullest without her here, just like the minister said at Mom's funeral. She wasn't able to do that, but she left gifts in each one of us so that we can.

And for that, I will always be grateful.

About the Author

Chynna lives in Edmonton, Alberta with her three daughters (Jaimie, eight; Jordhan, six; and Sophie, two) and baby boy, Xander (four). Her passion is helping children and families living with Sensory Processing Disorder and other special needs. Chynna just completed work at Athabasca University for a B.A. in Psychology, specializing in Early Childhood Development and children with special needs.

You'll find her work in many online and in-print parenting, inspirational, Christian and writing publications in Canada, United States, Australia, and Britain. In addition, she's authored *Not Just Spirited: A Mother's Sensational Journey With Sensory Processing Disorder* and a children's book, *I'm Not Weird, I Have SPD.*

Visit Chynna's websites to see the exciting work Chynna is doing now, as her grandparents predicted. They include www.LilyWolfWords.ca (named for her grandparents Lillian and Wilf Batty) and SeeTheWhiteElephants.blogspot.com, the White Elephants blog for families living with bipolar disorder.

Acknowledgements

A project like this doesn't happen without the encouragement, inspiration and love of some very phenomenal people. Here is my "Thank You" list:

To Cam: Thank you for giving me a reason to live through our childhood. Without your presence during those early years, I doubt I'd have made it to our teens.

To Uncle Craig and Dorothy: you have been my sources of strength my entire life. I appreciate your shoot-from-the-hip honesty, your guidance, your support and your undying love. Words can't express my gratitude to both of you.

To Grandpa and Grandma: I feel your presence each and every day. I know you are both still guiding my every footstep. I love and miss you terribly. I hope you are proud! (PS: I know I dream about you when

White Elephants

I'm *not* paying attention so thank you for being there even now!!)

To Auntie Lois: Thank you for teaching me that love doesn't have to hurt and that I am worthy of it. You filled my heart and gave me hope to keep moving forward.

To my small handful of dear friends: You know who you are! I appreciate your support and love through thick and thin. Without your unconditional love, I'd never have had the courage to put this story into print.

To Dad, Robin and the rest of my family: I am so happy we were given another chance. I'm sorry we weren't able to be the family we should have been but we, at least, have the ability to make new paths now. That's very powerful and I'm so grateful for that chance.

To the phenomenal ladies at Eagle Wings Press: Thank you from the bottom of my heart for believing in my story and for helping me tell it properly. You are the most amazing group of talented, beautifully-hearted and strong women I have come to know.

To Steve and my four little beauties: You are my life and my reason for contin-uing my journey. You have given me the strength to tell this story. Thank you for tolerating nights of sitting in Mama's lap while she wrote or edited; for occasional times when you had to stare at the back of my head waiting for me to finish a chapter so we could play, and for inspiring me to keep moving forward. How fortunate am I?

And to Mom: Thank you for giving me gifts of creativity and music. I continue to celebrate the "real" you through these talents. I hope I have done your story justice. No matter what the reader takes from this story, people need to know that you were a person *first*...perhaps a person we needed to figure out how to help. Or maybe the story is about finding the strength to try when you don't know what to do. I only hope other families are helped through our story.

Other books by
Chynna T. Laird

Not Just Spirited:
A Mother's Sensational Journey With Sensory Processing Disorder (SPD)
Loving Healing Press (November, 2009)

I'm Not Weird, I Have SPD
Outskirts Press (August, 2009)

Blackbird Flies
Astraea Press (Coming Spring, 2011)

Other books from
Eagle Wings Press
imprint of Silver Boomer Books

Slender Steps to Sanity
Twelve-Step Notes of Hope
by OAStepper, Compulsive Overeater
May, 2009

Writing Toward the Light
A Grief Journey
by Laura Flett
July, 2009

A Time for Verse
poetic ponderings on Ecclesiastes
by Barbara B. Rollins
December, 2009

Survived to Love
by Ed H
August, 2010

A Cloud of Witnesses
Two Big Books and Us
by Barbara B. Rollins
with OAStepper, Compulsive Overeater
coming March, 2011

Books from
Silver Boomer Books:

Silver Boomers
prose and poetry by and about baby boomers
March, 2008

Freckles to Wrinkles
August, 2008

This Path
September, 2009

Song of County Roads
by Ginny Greene
September, 2009

From the Porch Swing
memories of our grandparents
July, 2010

Flashlight Memories
coming February, 2011

Books from
Laughing Cactus Press
imprint of Silver Boomer Books

Poetry Floats
New and selected Philosophy-lite
by Jim Wilson
August, 2009

Bluebonnets, Boots and Buffalo Bones
by Sheryl L. Nelms
September, 2009

not so GRIMM
gentle fables and cautionary tales
by Becky Haigler
November, 2009

Three Thousand Doors
Karen Elaine Greene
August 2010

Milagros
by Tess Almendárez Lojacono
February, 2011